Grade 6

ADVANTAGE Grammar

Table of Contents

Table of Contents

CREDITS

Concept Development: Kent Publishing Services, Inc.

Written by: Dawn Purney

Editor: Thomas Hatch

Design/Production: Signature Design Group, Inc.

Art Director: Tom Cochrane

Project Director: Carolea Williams

Introduction

The **Advantage Grammar** series for grades 3-8 offers instruction and practice in key writing skills, including

- grammar and usage
- capitalization and punctuation
- spelling
- writing good sentences
- writing good paragraphs
- editing your work

Take a look at all the advantages this grammar series offers . . .

Strong Skill Instruction

- The teaching component at the top of each lesson provides the support students need to work through the book independently.

- Plenty of skill practice pages will ensure students master essential skills they need to become competent writers.

- Examples, models, and practice activities use content from across the curriculum so students are learning about social studies, science, and literature as they master writing skills.

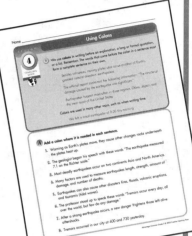

Editing Your Work pages provide for mixed practice of skills in a format that supports today's process approach to the teaching of writing.

Take a Test Drive pages provide practice using a test-taking format such as those included in national standardized and proficiency tests.

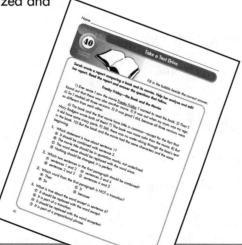

Name _____

Understanding Linking and Helping Verbs

 A **Linking verb** connects a noun to a description, usually an adjective or another noun.

Matter **is** all around.   Properties **are** characteristics of a thing.

Using certain pronouns with linking verbs may sound funny to us because we don't use them correctly in everyday speech.

Incorrect: This is **him**.   Correct: This is **he**.

Linking verbs often are forms of the verb "to be," but they can also relate to the five senses.

Some matter **is** rough.   Some matter **smells** like rotten eggs.

A **Circle the linking verb in the sentence.**

1. One property is an object's color.

2. Transparency is how much light passes through an object.

3. Most glass seems completely transparent.

4. Some things become harder or softer.

5. Fracturing and cleaving are ways matter breaks apart.

6. Matter tastes different.

7. Some rocks seem like something they are not!

8. Some glass grows cloudy over time.

B **Complete each sentence with a pronoun.**

1. The woman you should speak with is _____ .

2. It is _____ who wants to see the movie.

3. Where are _____ ?

A **helping verb** is used with a main verb to express time or mood.

   He **did** find the gold himself.   I **will** dig with him next time.

There may be more than one helping verb in a sentence.

   We **had been** thinking about it for awhile.

Sometimes a helping verb is not next to the main verb. Watch out for adverbs (words that modify verbs).

The   scientist   **had**   often   worked   late.   **Will**   he   be   home   soon?
              | | | | | |
          helping   adverb   main   helping noun main
           verb   verb   verb   verb

C **Underline the helping verbs and circle the main verb.**

1. Some metals can be made more magnetic.

2. We have been heating this mixture to find the boiling point.

3. We had found its melting point by accident.

4. They may have weighed it at the shop.

5. Next, our teacher will pour acid on a piece.

6. Did you experiment on that rock already?

7. It would quickly break apart.

8. A mixture might not completely mix.

9. Do not start yet!

10. We must review our safety rules first.

Name _____

⭐ Singular subjects need singular verbs. Generally, add an -s or –es to a regular verb to make it agree with a singular subject.

A liquid mix**es** more easily than a solid.
Our teacher show**s** us new experiments.

Plural subjects need plural verbs. If there are helping verbs, the first one is plural.

Gases mix even better!
Those measuring cups **have** been gone.

A **Determine whether the subject and predicate are singular or plural. Write *S* for singular and *P* for plural.**

1. ____ Many things are possible when mixing chemicals.

2. ____ Eventually water wears almost anything away!

3. ____ Some chemicals separate when combined.

4. ____ A mineral may change color when mixed with another.

5. ____ Certain mixes often give explosive results!

6. ____ This mix does not change quickly.

B **Circle the verb that matches the noun.**

1. Salt   do   does   dissolve in water.

2. You   know   knows   that water is a mix itself.

3. Some mixes   is   are   called compounds.

4. Only a chemical reaction   break   breaks   down a compound.

5. The chemical reaction   make   makes   an interesting display.

6. Safety goggles   is   are   required for this experiment!

Advantage Grammar Grade 6 © 2005 Creative Teaching Press

⭐ Some plurals don't end in –s, but they are still plural.

Children walk home from school.   **Geese swim** in our pond.

Some nouns may end with -s, but are not plural.

The **news is** great!   **Gymnastics is** harder than it looks.

Some nouns talk about a group as a whole, so they are singular.

My **family enjoys** swimming.   That **band is** new.

C **Write a sentence using the noun in the form it is given.**

1. (Women) _____
_____

2. (group) _____
_____

3. (mathematics) _____
_____

4. (pants) _____
_____

5. (mice) _____
_____

6. (crowd) _____
_____

D **Write sentences using the singular form and the plural form of the noun.**

1. (Men) _____
_____
_____

2. (class) _____
_____
_____

Name _____

3

PHYSICAL
SCIENCE

Subjects and Predicates

⭐ There may be several nouns in a sentence, but only one is the **simple subject**. The subject is the "do-er" or the "be-er" in the sentence. The object of a preposition cannot be the subject of a sentence.

Certain **minerals** are used in fireworks.
Factories grind the rocks into powder.
Each of the different colors is made with different minerals.

Likewise, there may be many verbs in a sentence, but only one simple predicate. The predicate is the action or state of being in a sentence.

All the powders **fit** into huge tubes so that they will remain dry.
Flares that are used as roadside warnings are also **considered** fireworks.

A Circle the simple subject of the sentence.

1. The color blue is made with copper.

2. Sodium becomes yellow in fireworks.

3. Rock powder is blended with others to create other combinations.

4. A compound of aluminum can make flash mixtures.

5. Have you ever seen a bad fireworks display?

B Underline the simple predicate of the sentence.

1. Pyrotechnicians are the people who set off the fireworks.

2. The job of pyrotechnicians has become safer recently.

3. For a long time, technicians lit fireworks by hand.

4. Now, firework companies use what is known as electrical matches.

5. Many companies fire fireworks with their computers.

Advantage Grammar Grade 6 © 2005 Creative Teaching Press

C **Circle the simple subject and underline the simple predicate.**

1. Nowadays, someone from the firework company designs the show with his computer.

2. A computer program allows him to input an entire show!

3. He must tell the computer the length of time between when the firework is fired and when it opens in the air.

4. If the show has music, that must be added in also.

5. The factory connects each firework to an electronic firing system.

6. The system can check for problems.

7. It reports any problems back to the computer.

8. Pyrotechnicians start the show with just the press of a button!

9. Of course, there is a "stop" button in case anything goes wrong.

10. Fireworks displays are now safer and more interesting.

11. Where do you watch fireworks on the Fourth of July?

12. What kind of system do they have?

LESSON

4

PHYSICAL
SCIENCE

Using Colons

⭐ We use **colons** in writing before an explanation, a long or formal quotation, or a list. The words that come before the colon in a sentence must form a complete sentence on their own.

> Mixes and compounds both come from substances that cannot be separated into simpler substances: elements.

> The textbook says: "Chemists use symbols to represent an element. 'O' stands for one atom of oxygen."

> You have probably heard of most of the elements, including the following: hydrogen, helium, carbon, sulfur, gold, and iron.

Colons are used in many other ways, such as when writing time.

> We begin science class at 1:15 every day.

A **Add a colon where it is needed to each sentence.**

1. Elements are divided into categories metallic, non-metallic, and carbon-based.

2. One element is found in all living things carbon.

3. One encyclopedia says "While it is only the fourteenth most common element on earth, carbons forms the most compounds by far."

4. Besides being in living things, carbon can be found in many other places, such as the following diamonds, coal, the sun, and the atmosphere.

5. There is a special on TV tonight about diamonds at 830.

B **Add a colon where it is needed. Be careful: Not every sentence will need a colon.**

1. If you looked at what makes up elements, you would have the smallest piece possible the atom.

2. There is really only one way to see atoms with a powerful microscope.

3. Atoms have protons and electrons.

4. At noon, we eat lunch, then we have science class.

Colons are used in E-mail messages and at the end of the greeting in a business letter.

> From: Tim <TimWard@sciencerus.com>
> To: Lisa <DandS@ford.edu>
> Subject: Your order
> Date: Thurs, Oct 14, 2004 3:45
>
> Dear Lisa Caraway:
> Your order has shipped. The Science Kit should arrive within 7-10 days.

Colons also separate titles from subtitles.

> Chemistry: Elemental Science

 Add colons where they are needed in this E-mail.

From: RaeAnn <msWizard@ruwo.com>

To: Lisa <DandS@ford.edu>

Subject chemistry workshop

Date Mon, Sept 6, 2004 9 30

Dear Mrs. Caraway

I'm looking forward to coming to your classroom Friday to give the chemistry workshop. Am I remembering that I can start setting up after 1200 and that we start class at 115?

Please send me the following items directions to your school, a list of your class's special interests, and any questions from your students about being a scientist. If you send the questions by Thursday, I can make an interesting presentation of the answers.

See you soon,

RaeAnn (Ms. Wizard)

5

PHYSICAL
SCIENCE

Suffixes

⭐ **Suffixes**, endings added to a word, can modify the meaning.

A tox**in** is a poison.   Tox**ic** means poisonous.

Suffixes can also determine how the word will function in the sentence.

Toxin is a noun.   **Toxic** is an adjective.

Study the following suffixes:

-ic – relating to

-ist – one connected with a certain action

-er – one who does a certain action

-istry – skill in

-ence or *-ance*; *-ency* or *-ancy* – thing having the quality or state of

-ent or *-ant* – having the quality or state of

A **Use the information above to match the italicized word with its definition. Be careful: There are more definitions than words to match.**

____ **1.** Be careful with that *sulfuric* acid!

____ **2.** The *chemist* will do the mixing for us.

____ **3.** A beaker is a special *container*.

____ **4.** If light passes through, it is a *transparency*.

a) being transparent

b) a transparent thing

c) skill with chemicals

d) a person working with chemicals

e) having sulfur

f) something that contains

B **Use the information in the box to write your own definition for each word.**

1. historic _____

2. artist _____

3. dentistry _____

4. announcer _____

5. appearance _____

6. infancy _____

Advantage Grammar Grade 6 © 2005 Creative Teaching Press

Use the clues to fill in the puzzle.

ACROSS

1. skill with chemicals

3. one who reports

7. relating to school

8. the act of assisting

9. the state of being constant

DOWN

1. the suffix meaning "having the quality"

4. people who plays the organ

5. the act of resisting

6. one who believes

D **Write a sentence using each word from the puzzle. Name the part of speech.**

_____ **1.** _____

_____

_____ **2.** _____

_____

_____ **3.** _____

_____

_____ **4.** _____

_____

_____ **5.** _____

_____

_____ **6.** _____

_____

_____ **7.** _____

_____

_____ **8.** _____

_____

_____ **9.** _____

PHYSICAL SCIENCE

Using Transitions

★ Transitions help sentences flow together better.

> We all know that liquids tend to flow better than solids. How matter flows is called its viscosity.

> We all know that liquids tend to flow better than solids. **This** is called its viscosity.

The word **this** connects the two sentences.

Transitional words and phrases also help connect ideas. Examples include phrases such as "for example," "of course," "finally," and "meanwhile."

A **Circle the transitional words and phrases in the paragraph.**

Since liquids flow, scientists can measure their viscosity. Sometimes you can tell how viscous a liquid is by how "thick" it looks. But many factors affect a liquid's viscosity. For instance, liquids are generally thicker at lower temperatures. In fact, most liquids can eventually become solids by freezing them. And the opposite is also true, the warmer the liquid, the thinner it becomes.

B **Complete the paragraph by writing a suitable transitional word or phrase in the blanks.**

Try this experiment to determine viscosity of household liquids. Collect the following: white grape juice, water colored with food coloring, corn syrup, liquid hand soap, baby oil, vegetable oil, marbles, and one clear glass for each liquid. _____ fill each glass with a different liquid. Make sure each glass has the same amount. _____ _____ you begin, predict which liquid is more viscous, or thick._____ drop a marble in each separate liquid. _____ compare your results with your predictions.

C Circle the 13 single transitional words in the puzzle. Use the letters left over to fill in the blanks below, and reveal the secret message.

_ _ _ _ _ _ _ _ _ _ _   _ _ _   _ _ _ _ ,   _ _ _   _ _ _ _ _   _ _ _

_ _ _   _ _ _ _ !

```
T   T   H   E   R   E   F   O   R   E
L   R   X   A   N   S   F   R   S   O
L   I   B   E   S   I   D   E   S   T
I   T   U   I   N   N   O   V   E   H
T   N   T   A   S   C   A   E   C   E
S   R   L   E   G   E   O   W   O   R
O   L   D   B   U   S   O   O   N   W
Y   A   T   D   O   N   O   H   D   I
T   S   U   S   E   T   O   O   M   S
A   T   H   O   U   G   H   N   Y   E
```

D Write your own paragraph using transitional words and phrases. You can use a topic below or one of your own.

How to build a....   A trip to the store   The best party ever

_____

_____

_____

_____

_____

_____

_____

7

PHYSICAL
SCIENCE

Editing Your Work

 Editing your work is an important step in the writing process. Many tests ask you to show what you know about editing.

A Rachel wrote a report about atoms. Help her revise and edit her report. Read the paragraphs and follow the directions.

Anatomy of an Atom

1) All matter is made of atoms. 2) Atoms are so small you can't see them. 3) Atoms have three basic parts: protons, neutrons, and electrons. 4) Protons have a positive charge and electrons have a negative charge. 5) It is a little like magnetic things. 6) The protons and neutrons make up the center of the atom. 7) Electrons circle around the center. 8) Electrons are much lighter than protons and neutrons.

9) The center of an atom is called the nucleus. 10) The nucleus contains a lot of energy. 11) When scientists learned how to use that energy, atomic energy was invented. 12) You may have heard it called something else: nuclear energy.

1. What is the linking and main verb in sentence 1?

   _____

2. Which verb is the simple predicate in sentence 1? _____

3. What is the simple subject and simple predicate for sentence 7?

   _____

4. What does the word *atomic* mean? _____

5. What does the word *magnetic* mean? _____

6. Which sentence contains a colon before an explanation? _____

7. Which sentence contains a colon before a list? _____

8. What is the simple subject and predicate in sentence 12?

   _____

Advantage Grammar Grade 6 © 2005 Creative Teaching Press

B Continue reading and editing Rachel's report.

1) If another proton joins the atom, it forms a new kind of atom!

2) Nitrogen, a common gas, has six protons. 3) If another one was added, the atom becomes something else: oxygen! 4) Once scientists learned about adding protons, they created brand-new atoms.

5) You can learn more about atoms using the science of chemistry. 6) If you really like chemistry, you might consider a career as a chemist. 7) Chemists can work in lots of places: pharmacies, food companies, or even power companies.

1. What is the simple subject and predicate in sentence 1? _____

2. Rewrite sentence 2, adding a transition to connect it to the sentence before it.

_____

_____

3. List the helping verbs from these sentences. 3) _____

5) _____   6) _____   7) _____

4. What does the word *chemistry* mean? _____

_____

5. How is the colon used in sentence 3?

_____

_____

6. Complete this rewrite of sentence 7, which changes the noun from plural to singular.
A chemist _____

_____

_____

_____

7. What does the word *one* in sentence 3 refer to?

_____

_____

Name _____

Take a Test Drive

Fill in the bubble beside the correct answer.

William wrote a report about oxygen. Help him revise and edit his report. Read the report and answer the questions that follow.

Oxygen

1) In science class, we learned that atoms make up elements. 2) You have probably heard of many elements, including the following: helium, iron, fluorine, copper, and calcium. 3) And we all know the most common element on Earth: oxygen.

4) Some may think of oxygen as the air around us, but oxygen is only part of our atmosphere. 5) Of course, to us humans who need the oxygen in the air, it is the most important part. 6) We breathe in the air and use the oxygen. 7) We breathe out the rest: this is called exhaling. 8) In fact, all living things—plants and animals— need oxygen to live. 9) Some animals breathe differently than us. 10) For example, fish get oxygen from the oxygen in water, not from the air. 11) But they would still die without it.

1. What is the simple subject in sentence 1?
   Ⓐ elements   Ⓒ class
   Ⓑ learned   Ⓓ we

2. Which is the helping verb in sentence 2?
   Ⓕ You   Ⓗ heard
   Ⓖ have   Ⓙ probably

3. Which sentence uses a colon to introduce a list?
   Ⓐ sentence 2   Ⓒ sentence 7
   Ⓑ sentence 3   Ⓓ none of the above

4. Which phrase is **not** a transitional phrase?
   Ⓕ In science class (sentence 1)
   Ⓖ For example (sentence 10)
   Ⓗ Of course (sentence 5)
   Ⓙ In fact (sentence 8)

Continue reading William's report. Answer the questions.

1) We know oxygen as a gas, but it can be a liquid or a solid as well. 2) Solid oxygen is not easy to make. 3) It is used mostly by scientists for experiments. 4) Liquid oxygen is used by the space program to cool the engines or even power the rockets. 5) Also, liquid oxygen is sometimes used for pilots and sick people who have trouble breathing. 6) But it can be dangerous, so it is used for one purpose: in an emergency!

7) In fact, oxygen can be damaging in several ways. 8) It can mix with almost anything, but sometimes these mixtures have reactions. 9) This is called oxidation. 10) Oxidation can mean anything from rusting to exploding. 11) And although it does not burn, oxygen must be there for something to be able to burn.

5. Which is the simple subject in sentence 5?
   - Ⓐ pilots
   - Ⓑ people
   - Ⓒ trouble
   - Ⓓ none of the above

6. Which sentence uses the word *is* as a linking verb?
   - Ⓕ sentence 2
   - Ⓖ sentence 4
   - Ⓗ sentence 5
   - Ⓙ sentence 9

7. William could have discussed oxidents in his report. Which definition best fits the word *oxidents*?
   - Ⓐ skill with oxygen
   - Ⓑ one who makes oxygen
   - Ⓒ one who works with oxygen
   - Ⓓ something with the qualities of oxygen

8. What word is the simple predicate in sentence 4?
   - Ⓕ power
   - Ⓖ cool
   - Ⓗ used
   - Ⓙ is

LESSON

9

WONDERS OF
THE NATURAL
WORLD

Compound Subject-Predicate Agreement

⭐ Sentences with more than one subject have **compound subjects**. Since a compound subject is plural, the predicate needs to be plural.

Singular Subject: The **harbor** of Rio de Janiero **is** one of the Seven Wonders of the Natural World.

Plural Subject: **Explorers thought** it was the mouth of a river.

Compound Subject: The **harbor** and the **city are** twenty miles inland from the coast of Brazil.

A Write *S* if the subject is singular and *P* if the subject is plural. Circle the predicate.

_____ **1.** The harbor is also called Guanabara Bay.

_____ **2.** Mountains surround the large waterway.

_____ **3.** Its name means the "River of January."

_____ **4.** An island and the hills make the harbor look like a lake.

_____ **5.** The beauty and uniqueness make this place a natural wonder.

B Circle the predicate that agrees with the subject.

1. A huge city   sit   sits   in the lowlands around the harbor.

2. Portuguese people   was   were   the first Europeans to explore the harbor.

3. The harbor, city, and state   is   are   all named Rio de Janeiro.

4. A giant statute   stands   stand   atop one of the mountains.

5. The Copacabana and Ipanema   is   are   famous beaches around the harbor.

6. Cable cars   takes   take   people to the top of one mountain.

7. Adventurers   hang-glides   hang-glide   down another mountain to a beach.

8. Every sightseer   has   have   many options of how to view the harbor!

⭐ Predicates can also be compound. All predicates must agree with the subject or compound subject.

> Brazilians **work** and **play** at the harbor.
> Cruise ships and tankers **dock** and **load** there.

C **Underline the subject or compound subject. Circle the predicate or compound predicate.**

1. Mountains jut up or slope into the ocean.
2. An airport is on the island in the harbor.
3. Heavy rains often cause landslides.
4. Of all South American countries, Brazil is the largest.
5. The flatland and some mountains house people and support skyscrapers.

D **Complete the sentence by writing the correct form of the predicate shown in parentheses.**

1. (be) The Amazon River and Rainforest _____ in Brazil.
2. (house) The tropical area _____ many unique creatures.
3. (live) Flesh-eating piranha fish _____ in the river.
4. (root, swim) Tapirs with a long nose _____ in the rainforest and _____ in the river.
5. (race) Freshwater dolphins _____ in the Amazon River.
6. (come) The raccoon-like kinkajou only _____ out at night.
7. (fly, squawk) A parrot with his colorful feathers _____ and _____ overhead.
8. (hunt) Ocelots of the cat family _____ in trees and on land.
9. (collect, create) Leafcutter ants _____ leaves and _____ their own fungus to eat.
10. (be) The huge rodents _____ named capybara.

LESSON

10

WONDERS OF
THE NATURAL
WORLD

Indefinite Pronouns

⭐ Although most pronouns stand for a noun that was already stated,
indefinite pronouns do not.

> **Everybody** should see the Grand Canyon.
> **No one** wants to see it more than I do!

Indefinite pronouns are always singular. Remember to also keep the predicate
singular, so that it agrees with the subject.

> **Everyone agrees** that it is a natural wonder.
> **None** of us **has** seen it yet.

A Circle the indefinite pronoun.

1. Anyone who has flown from the East Coast to the West Coast has
   probably seen it.

2. The beauty and adventure of the Canyon would appeal to anybody.

3. Someone I knew took a mule ride to the bottom of the Grand Canyon.

4. You should ask somebody else to take the raft trip with you!

5. Nobody could possibly see the whole thing.

6. One would think the task impossible.

7. Some may come to simply view the huge hole from above.

8. Several of my friends camped near the canyon in Arizona.

9. Few visit Arizona in the summer.

10. But park rangers say that there's no day that no one comes.

11. You can hike or ride down, but I like to do neither.

12. My sister would like to try everything there is to do there.

13. Grand Canyon National Park is free to all who come.

14. Something tells me that you want to go there too!

Advantage Grammar Grade 6 © 2005 Creative Teaching Press

⭐ Using other pronouns with indefinite pronouns can be confusing.

Everyone should bring **his** lunch along.
Everyone should bring **his** or **her** lunch along.

In informal speech and writing, Americans often use the word **their** to avoid male and female pronouns. Do not do this in formal situations.

Informal: **Each** must remember **their** sunscreen.
Formal: **Each** must remember **his** sunscreen.
            Each must remember **his** or **her** sunscreen.

B **Create your own sentences using indefinite pronouns.**

_____

_____

_____

_____

_____

_____

_____

_____

_____

_____

_____

_____

_____

_____

_____

LESSON

11

WONDERS OF
THE NATURAL
WORLD

Dependent and Independent Clauses

★ An **independent clause** has a subject and a predicate. It can stand alone as a complete sentence and still make sense.

> The Northern Lights is not a certain place, it is something that happens in a certain place.

> The Northern Lights is not a certain place. It is something that happens in a certain place.

A **dependent clause** has a subject and a predicate, but it cannot stand alone because it is not a complete sentence.

> **When one is close to the North Pole,** one can see the Northern Lights.

A Label each clause with **IC** for independent clause or **DC** for dependent clause.

_____ **1.** The sun sends out a stream of protons and electrons.

_____ **2.** Because they are attracted to Earth's magnetic poles.

_____ **3.** As colored lights arc across the sky.

B Label each clause with **IC** for independent clause or **DC** for dependent clause.

1. The sun has storms,   just like planet Earth.
  _____   _____

2. During the spring and fall,   the sun storms are usually the worst.
  _____   _____

3. The sun sends out protons and electrons,   which is called the solar wind.
  _____   _____

4. When the solar wind reaches Earth,   it is attracted to the magnetic poles.
  _____   _____

5. As the solar wind meets our atmosphere,   arcs of colored fill the sky.
  _____   _____

Name _____

 Some dependent clauses appear in the middle of a sentence.

Alaska, <u>which is the northernmost state</u>, is a great place to see Northern Lights.
dependent clause

Some sentences do not have any dependent clauses.

<u>Sometimes the Lights are in shades of red</u>, and <u>sometimes they are in shades of blue</u>.
independent clause   independent clause

In some sentences, the dependent clause makes up the subject or completes the predicate.

<u>Clouds covering the sky</u> can block your view of the Lights.
dependent clause as the subject

The color of the Lights depends on <u>how high they are in the sky</u>.
dependent clause completing the predicate

C **Write the number of independent clauses in each sentence. Underline each dependent clause. Remember: Not every sentence will have a dependent clause.**

_____ **1.** If you find a place with little artificial light, it's the best area to see the Lights.

_____ **2.** Sometimes, the Lights can be seen from even further away than close to the poles.

_____ **3.** The Northern Lights are also called the *Aurora Borealis*, and the Southern Lights are called the *Aurora Australis*.

_____ **4.** One might think that the photos of the Lights aren't real.

_____ **5.** The few people on Antarctica often see spectacular shows of the Southern Lights.

_____ **6.** I must tell you that we can't see the Lights here often.

_____ **7.** Perfect conditions to see them include a clear sky.

_____ **8.** The Lights take on the form of many shapes, such as curtains or arcs of light.

Using Commas and Semicolons

WONDERS OF THE NATURAL WORLD

⭐ One way to connect independent clauses is to use a comma and a short conjunction such as *and, but, or, yet, for, so, nor.*

Mt. Everest is the tallest mountain on Earth, **and** it is a Natural Wonder.

A Add a comma in the correct place.

1. The Himalayan Mountain range is known for being in Nepal but it also borders China.

2. The country is a kingdom yet it also has a prime minister as well.

3. Kathmandu is the capital city and it is also its largest and most famous city.

4. Nepal has a subtropical climate for it is the same distance from the equator as Florida.

5. It has a mild climate so the only snow Nepal sees is in the mountains.

B Add a comma in sentences with independent clauses connected by short conjunctions.

1. Mt. Everest is in the country of Nepal in Asia.

2. The air gets thinner as land gets higher.

3. The Sherpa people of Nepal are more used to the thinner air so they have an easier time climbing in higher elevations.

4. New Zealand adventurer Edmund Hillary decided to climb with Sherpa Tenzing Norgay.

5. The men were the first to climb to the top of the mountain and they will always be remembered for this feat.

> ★ To connect two independent clauses without a conjunction, use a semicolon.
>
> Sir Edmund Hillary climbed Mt. Everest; he also led a journey to the South Pole.

C **Add a semicolon in the correct place.**

1. Sir Edmund Hillary wrote books about his adventures you can read about most of his trips.

2. Hillary was knighted by Queen Elizabeth II he could then add Sir to his name.

3. Hillary and Norgay climbed together neither ever said who actually stepped to the summit first.

D **Rewrite as one sentence. You may either use a semicolon or a comma and a conjunction.**

1. Hillary and Norgay found George Mallory's body on their climb. They couldn't tell if Mallory had reached the summit or not.

   _____
   _____
   _____
   _____

2. Tenzing Norgay had tried many times to reach the summit of Mt. Everest. He probably spent more time on the mountain than anyone else in history!

   _____
   _____
   _____
   _____

3. Tenzing Norgay passed away in 1986. Sir Hillary is still alive.

   _____
   _____
   _____
   _____

Name _____

Organizing by Alphabetical Order

⭐ Compare the first letter of each word first to find which comes first alphabetically.

Indian Ocean - Pacific Ocean

Compare the second letters if the first letters are the same. Then compare the third letters, and so on.

Zambia - Zimbabwe   Alaska - Arizona - Arkansas

A Number each place name to show alphabetical order.

1. ____ Grand Canyon   ____ Great Barrier Reef

2. ____ Himalayas   ____ Highlands

3. ____ Mt. Everest   ____ Mt. Darwin   ____ Mt. Dade

4. ____ Greenland   ____ Finland   ____ Canada   ____ Norway

5. ____ Kone   ____ Kos   ____ Kilauea   ____ Krakatoa

B Rewrite each list in alphabetical order.

1. volcano, mountain, waterfall, canyon, reef, harbor _____

_____

2. Albania, Austria, Australia, Armenia, Argentina, Angola _____

_____

3. Anguilla, Bermuda, Barbados, Aruba, Antigua, Barbuda, Bahamas

_____

_____

_____

4. Virginia, Washington, Vermont, Wisconsin, West Virginia, Wyoming

_____

_____

_____

⭐ Abbreviated words are listed in alphabetical order as if they were spelled out.
ID comes before IA because I̲daho comes before I̲owa.

C **Match the abbreviation with the word it represents. Hint: Some abbreviations stand for more than one thing.**

_____ 1. Mt.   _____ 5. Capt.   A. Missus   F. Captain
                                              B. Mister   G. Mountain
_____ 2. St.   _____ 6. Mr.   C. West   H. Saint
                                              D. Street   I. Doctor
_____ 3. N.   _____ 7. Mrs.   E. North   J. Mount
_____ 4. W.   _____ 8. Dr.

D **Number the words to show alphabetical order.**

1. ____ Mt. Adams   ____ Mount McKinley ____ Pikes Peak   ____ Mauna Loa

2. ____ St. Louis   ____ South Bend   ____ San Antonio   ____ Seattle

3. ____ Mr. Adams   ____ Mrs. Downs   ____ Mister Wilson ____ Miss Banks

4. ____ Wall St.   ____ Wall Avenue   ____ Wall South   ____ South Way

5. ____ Mammoth Mt.   ____ Mt. Hood   ____ Mt. St. Helens ____ Mount Shasta

E **Rewrite the list in alphabetical order.**

1. Brazil, U.S.A., Mexico, Zambia, Australia, Nepal _____

_____

2. Mt. Everest, Victoria Falls, Grand Canyon, Great Barrier Reef, Northern Lights, Harbor of Rio de Janeiro, Paracutin Volcano _____

_____

_____

Chronological Order

14

WONDERS OF
THE NATURAL
WORLD

 Arranging a paragraph in time order, or the sequence in which things happen, is called using **chronological order**.

Words that help show chronological order are shown in bold.

> **In the mid-1800s,** a medical missionary named David Livingstone was living in Africa. He traveled down the Zambezi River. He learned a lot about the area along the way. **At the end of his journey**, Livingstone found a wonderful surprise: a huge waterfall. He was the first person outside of the natives to see what he named Victoria Falls.

Transition words, such as **first**, **finally**, and **next** can also help the reader keep track of the order.

A **Rewrite the facts listed below as a paragraph. Use words to help show chronological order.**

Even today, getting to Victoria Falls isn't quick or easy.
Get yourself to New York City.
Fly to Dakar, Senegal.
Fly to the capital of South Africa, Johannesburg.
Take a train up to Livingstone, Zimbabwe.
Take a bus, rental car, or hike to Victoria Falls.
Hike across a bridge to enter Zambia and see the falls from both countries!

_____

_____

_____

_____

_____

_____

_____

Advantage Grammar Grade 6 © 2005 Creative Teaching Press

B Number each sentence to show the order the sentences should appear.

_____ While looking for the source of the Nile, he lost several companions.

_____ Years after he told the world about Victoria Falls, Livingstone was still exploring Africa.

_____ Then, in 1866, Livingstone decided to look for the source of the Nile River.

_____ He also lost contact with the outside word.

C Rewrite the facts above as a paragraph in chronological order.

_____

_____

_____

_____

_____

_____

D Number each sentence to show the order the sentences should appear.

_____ It took a year for Stanley to find Livingstone.

_____ When the two men met, Stanley tipped his hat and said the now-famous words, "Dr. Livingstone, I presume."

_____ In 1869, a reporter named Henry Stanley set out to search for the explorer and bring him supplies.

E Rewrite the facts above as a paragraph in chronological order.

_____

_____

_____

_____

_____

_____

_____

Editing Your Work

 Editing your work is an important step in the writing process. Many tests ask you to show what you know about editing.

 A **Justin wrote a report about a natural wonder. Help him revise and edit his report. Read the report and answer the questions that follow.**

Instant Volcano

1) Not far from Mexico City, a volcano sprung up overnight. 2) For weeks, the townspeople had heard what sounded like thunder. 3) But the skies were always clear. 4) One day, a farmer and his wife heard a hissing sound in their cornfield. 5) When they looked, they saw a crack in the ground. 6) As they watched, they heard the "thunder" again, then the ground began to swell up. 7) Ashes, smoke, and rocks, came out of the crack.

8) By the next day, the cone grew as high as a house. 9) Within a week, it doubled in size. 10) The field and the town was covered in ashes. 11) Lava also covered other surrounding towns. 12) Ashes fell as far as two hundred miles away. 13) Nobody could live there anymore.

1. Rewrite sentences 2 and 3 as one sentence. _____

   _____

   _____

2. Which two sentences in the first paragraph have a compound subject? _____

   _____

3. Which word in the second paragraph is an indefinite pronoun? _____

4. Rewrite sentence 10 to make the subject and verb agree. _____

   _____

5. What is the dependent clause in sentence 6? _____

   _____

6. Write a number beside each volcano name to show alphabetical order.

   ___ Paricutin ___ Pacaya ___ Mt. St. Helens ___ Mauna Loa ___Mount Schank

 Advantage Grammar Grade 6 © 2005 Creative Teaching Press

Name _____

B **Continue revising and editing Justin's report.**

1) <u>Over the next nine years,</u> the volcano became a mountain. 2) Several were killed by lightning that was caused by the volcano. 3) One of the last eruptions killed 1,000 more. 4) Many moved away to start new lives.

5) But now, Paricutin Volcano is safe. 6) It is no longer active. 7) The ash made the field even better for growing crops. 8) The volcano is one of the Seven Wonders of the Natural World. 9) Tourists come to see the volcano. 10) One reason Paricutin is so famous is because people saw it from start to finish. 11) It happened in the 1900s so its eruptions were captured on film.

1. Why isn't the underlined phrase in sentence 1, a clause? _____
   _____
   _____

2. Which word in sentence 2 is an indefinite pronoun? _____

3. Rewrite sentences 5 and 6 as one sentence.
   _____
   _____
   _____

4. Where should a comma be placed in sentence 11?
   _____

5. Which sentence has a dependent clause that completes the subject of the sentence? _____

6. Rewrite the following words in alphabetical order:

   seven   wonders   of   the   natural   world

   _____
   _____

7. Which words or phrases in the report tell about chronological order?
   _____
   _____
   _____

LESSON

16

WONDERS OF THE NATURAL WORLD

Take a Test Drive

Fill in the bubble beside the correct answer.

Kelsey wrote a report about another natural wonder. Help her revise and edit her report. Read the report and answer the questions that follow.

The Great Barrier Reef

1) Off the coast of Australia is the largest natural structure on Earth: the Great Barrier Reef. 2) It is 1250 miles long and gets up to 90 miles wide! 3) Reefs are made when certain coral animals connect their hard bodies together. 4) The reefs are close to the surface of the water. 5) In fact, the top of a coral reef may stick up out of the water when the tide is out.

6) One may think that coral look like plants or even rocks, but they are really animals. 7) They cannot move. 8) Yet they have everything they need. 9) This is partly because many other animals live in and visit the reef. 10) The reefs offer protection for many fish. 11) The amount of sea life there makes the Reef one of Earth's most important places. 12) Everyone should see the Great Barrier Reef!

1. Which is **not** an indefinite pronoun?
   Ⓐ one
   Ⓒ everyone
   Ⓑ they
   Ⓓ none of the above

2. Which phrase is an independent clause?
   Ⓕ is the largest structure on Earth
   Ⓖ close to the surface of the water
   Ⓗ they are really animals
   Ⓙ when the tide is out

3. Which two sentences could be made into one by changing a period to a semicolon?
   Ⓐ sentences 3 & 4
   Ⓒ sentences 6 & 7
   Ⓑ sentences 4 & 5
   Ⓓ sentences 7 & 8

4. Which sentence has a compound predicate?
   Ⓕ sentence 4
   Ⓗ sentence 9
   Ⓖ sentence 5
   Ⓙ sentence 11

Continue revising and editing Kelsey's report.

1) Hard corals make the reefs. 2) The individual animals are called polyps. 3) First a polyp must be in warm, clear waters. 4) They take calcium from the ocean water and use it to form a hard cup. 5) As the polyps grow, they form colonies. 6) The colonies branch out and grow. 7) Soon other living things join them. 8) For example, algae can live right on the coral. 9) Many fish dwell among their branches. 10) When a polyp dies, the body remains, and others grows around it. 11) This is how the Great Barrier Reef grew so big.

5. Which phrase does not show chronological order?
- Ⓐ As they grow
- Ⓒ First
- Ⓑ For example
- Ⓓ Soon

6. Which list is in alphabetical order?
- Ⓕ grew, great, grow, algae, coral
- Ⓖ algae, coral, grew, great, grow
- Ⓗ coral, algae, great, grew, grow
- Ⓙ algae, coral, great, grew, grow

7. Which rewrite of sentences 8 and 9 combines them correctly?
- Ⓐ For example, algae can live right on the coral, and many fish dwell among their branches.
- Ⓑ For example, algae can live right on the coral; and many fish dwell among their branches.
- Ⓒ For example, algae can live right on the coral, many fish dwell among their branches.
- Ⓓ For example, algae can live right on the coral; Many fish dwell among their branches.

8. How should sentence 10 be corrected?
- Ⓕ change a comma to a semicolon
- Ⓖ change the word grows to grow
- Ⓗ change the word dies to die
- Ⓙ it is already correct

9. Which phrase from sentence 4 is the dependent clause?
- Ⓐ They take calcium
- Ⓑ from the ocean water
- Ⓒ use it to form a hard cup
- Ⓓ none of the above, there is no dependent clause

Name _____

Identifying Infinitives

⭐ An **infinitive** is formed by the word *to* and the root of a verb.

We want **to study** organisms.

A **Underline the infinitive in the sentence.**

1. An organism has organs and other parts that work together to keep it alive.

2. What else will help to decide if something is an organism?

3. Whether it is plant, animals, or fungus, an organism's main goal is to survive.

4. Most organisms will do unusual things to continue living.

5. Plants cannot move but will grow toward the light to be sure to get enough light.

6. Many plants have defensive parts to protect them from harm.

B **Write the letter of the infinitive that best completes the sentence.**

1. An organism needs _____ parts that do more than one thing.

2. Cells function together _____ one thing for the body, such as change food into energy.

3. Cells join together _____ one organ.

4. Each organ, such as an animal's heart, has its own task _____ the organism alive.

5. _____ about organisms, divide them into groups, such as plants and animals.

6. _____ at micro-organisms, one needs a microscope.

a) to do
b) to study
c) to keep
d) to look
e) to have
f) to form

Name _____

 The word *to* is used many different ways. It can be part of an infinitive, or a preposition.

     infinitive: First we needed **to identify** what organisms are.

     preposition: Learning about life forms is interesting **to** me.

Sometimes the parts of an infinitive are separated by an adverb.

     I will try to **secretly** borrow one from my grandfather.
     He's so hard of hearing, it's easier to **not** ask him.

C **Underline the 5 infinitives. Hint: Two sentences have no infinitive, but another has two.**

1. To find a good definition is our goal.

2. Most scientists like to divide organisms into categories.

3. Look for certain traits to decide in which category an organism fits.

4. Please bring the mushroom to my house later.

5. We may need to use a magnifying glass to examine it closely.

6. Be sure that it is pinned to the mat first.

D **Underline the infinitives.**

1. We want to use the microscope to see what's in water.

2. You need to carefully drop the water on the slide.

3. Be careful to not let air get trapped in there too.

4. Many people think they need to squint when using a microscope.

5. Grandpa would have told us to keep both eyes open.

6. Will you help me take it back to him when we're done?

LESSON

18

PLANTS AND
ANIMALS

Using Prepositional Phrases

⭐ A **prepositional phrase** shows how things are related, gives time and place information, or tells a condition.

near the desk   until the show   except for you   without a care

A prepositional phrase always ends with a noun. The word that begins a prepositional phrase is the preposition.

beyond the limits   **until** then   **of** the house

A **Underline the prepositional phrases in each sentence. Some sentences may have more than one.**

1. I put a plant on the windowsill.

2. There is dirt and a seed in the pot.

3. There is another plant beneath the stairs.

4. It is not in front of a window.

5. We will watch what happens to a plant with sunlight and without it.

6. During our experiment, we will not move the plants.

7. I used plants of the same kind.

8. There should be no difference except for the amount of sunlight.

B **Underline the prepositional phrases and circle the prepositions.**

1. After our first experiment, we will do another one.

2. We must keep track of our plants over time.

3. Besides our notes, we could also take pictures of each pot.

4. We haven't missed one day since the beginning.

Name _____

> ★ The word *to* can begin a prepositional phrase or an infinitive. Remember: a prepositional phrase ends with a noun and an infinitive ends with a verb.
>
> We need   to go   to the greenhouse.
>   infinitive   prepositional phrase

C **Write *P* if the word *to* is used as a preposition and underline the noun in the phrase. Write *I* if the word *to* is used as an infinitive and circle the verb.**

_____ 1. I must go between them to take notes.

_____ 2. We should go to the store.

_____ 3. I need to get another plant.

_____ 4. To the garden it will go.

_____ 5. Our plant smells bad according to Mom.

_____ 6. In addition to the plant growing here, there's another over there.

_____ 7. We were lucky to have one already.

_____ 8. I would like to ask you a question.

D **Write one sentence using *to* in a prepositional phrase, and one using *to* in an infinitive.**

Preposition:

_____

_____

_____

Infinitive:

_____

_____

_____

Name _____

Simple, Compound, and Complex Sentences

⭐ A **simple sentence** has one independent clause. It does not matter how many adjective, adverbs, infinitives, and prepositional phrases there are.

An ecosystem is a collection of living things and their environment.

A **compound sentence** has two independent clauses.

Ecosystems include a physical place, and it also includes plants and animals there.

A Write *Simple* if the sentence is a simple sentence. Write *Compound* if it is a compound sentence.

_____ **1.** Some plants can live with very little light, but none can survive without any.

_____ **2.** No plants live in the depths of the ocean.

_____ **3.** Plants on the rainforest floor only get filtered sunlight.

_____ **4.** Direct sun may kill some plants; shade kills others.

_____ **5.** Some plants are hardy; they can adapt to sun or shade.

_____ **6.** On the other hand, some plants are more sensitive than others.

B Write your own sentences.

Simple sentence:

_____

_____

Compound sentence:

_____

_____

Name _____

⭐ A **complex sentence** has a dependent clause. It also has at least one independent clause.

Some fish live so deep in the ocean <u>that they get no light from the sun</u>.
          independent clause   dependent clause

C Write *Simple* if the sentence is a simple sentence. Write *Compound* if it is a compound sentence. Write *Complex* if it is a complex sentence. Underline the dependent clause.

_____ 1. Every animal needs light to live.

_____ 2. Some fish in the deep create their own light in order to see.

_____ 3. When an animal creates its own light, it is said to be bioluminescent.

_____ 4. The anglerfish uses a glowing limb to attract prey; some call it their fishing pole.

_____ 5. The angler has long fin rays to sense other fish around it.

_____ 6. Some fish take advantage of being in the dark.

_____ 7. Gulper eels have black skin, which helps them hide in darkness.

_____ 8. Although they may never see light themselves, deep-sea fish feed off waste from animals above that do see light.

D Write your own complex sentence.

_____

_____

_____

_____

Using Hyphens

20

PLANTS AND
ANIMALS

⭐ Use a hyphen between the tens word and ones word for numbers twenty-one through ninety-nine.

      thirty-five   sixty-two   eighty-nine

Also use hyphens with fractions.

      one-half   five-sixths   two-thirds

Use a hyphen to break words between lines. Place the hyphen between syllables.

    re-   punc-   environ-
    flex   tuation   ment

A Add hyphens where they are missing.

  1. forty six _____

  2. three fourths _____

  3. nineteen _____

  4. three hundred _____

  5. one hundred fifty six _____

  6. seven eighths _____

B Place a hyphen between syllables.

  1. h y p h e n a t e   **6.** o r g a n i s m

  2. s h o r t   **7.** c e l l

  3. u n i t   **8.** g r a m m a r

  4. s i m p l e   **9.** s e n t e n c e

  5. c o m p o u n d   **10.** p a r a g r a p h s

⭐ Use a hyphen after a prefix if it is followed by a proper noun or proper adjective.

mid-August   Afro-American   pre-Egyptian

Use a hyphen with the prefix *all-*, *self-*, and *ex-* (meaning "former").

all-knowing   self-rising   ex-convict

C **If the word needs a hyphen, rewrite it with the hyphen in the correct place.**

1. midweek _____

2. preReagan _____

3. selftaught _____

4. prehistoric _____

5. midMarch _____

6. exwife _____

7. postCanadian _____

8. midday _____

9. selfseeking _____

10. expresident _____

11. allinclusive _____

12. nonBritish _____

D **Brainstorm a list of words that fit the rules above.**

_____

_____

_____

_____

Spelling Compounds with a Hyphen

21

PLANTS AND
ANIMALS

⭐ Use a hyphen to connect two or more words that are used as one word.

well-made shirt   **red-hot** coals

Use a hyphen when a noun is being used as an adjective.

I will use it **one time**. It is for **one-time** use only.
       noun   adjective

Use a hyphen when a verb is used as a noun.

He would **mock up** a model first.
      verb
This small boat is a **mock-up** of his big one.
      noun

A **Underline the two words that should be a temporary compound and add the hyphen.**

1. I will put on my push up leggings to walk in the swamp.

2. Cutting through these weeds is a full time job.

3. They flight test an airplane before taking passengers.

4. A turtle may be slow on land, but it becomes a high speed swimmer in water.

5. His shell is a bluish grey color.

6. This man's job is basically as a go between for other companies.

7. His company wants to buy a fifty yard wide field.

8. They will go with the highest priced offer.

Advantage Grammar Grade 6 © 2005 Creative Teaching Press

⭐ When modifying words come after a noun, they are generally not hyphenated.

We used **fire-resistant** cloth to make the curtains **fire resistant**.

A person's age is not hyphenated when it appears after the noun. Hyphenate if the words come before the noun and when they are used as a noun.

I am **twelve years old**.   I am a **twelve-year-old** girl.   The **twelve-year-old** won.

B **Put a checkmark before the sentence that needs a hyphen added. Add the hyphen.**

1. _____ a) The tour company was first rate.

   _____ b) Tara is a first rate tour guide.

2. _____ a) Nobody younger than six years old could come.

   _____ b) It was a six year old boat.

3. _____ a) The monkey has a higher up rank in his troop.

   _____ b) The snake was higher up than the monkey.

4. _____ a) A three year old was my favorite monkey.

   _____ b) His mother was a ten year old.

5. _____ a) They sat on a two foot long branch.

   _____ b) At least it seemed two feet long.

C **Explain how the hyphen makes the sentences different in meaning.**

Grandpa Smith was an old furniture seller.

Grandpa Smith was an old-furniture seller.

_____

_____

_____

Name _____

Cause and Effect

⭐ Cause and effect paragraphs show how one event brings on another one.

Words that signal causes or effects in the paragraph below are in bold.

Gardeners can use the environment to control their plants. For example, **when** the weather is cooler, some plants **become** dormant. A dormant plant does not grow as much, **therefore** you do not need to water it as much either. In fact, **if** you water the plant too much, **then** you could drown it! Some gardeners will put the plant in a cool place **in order to** fool it into becoming dormant. The plant "thinks" it is time to bloom again **once** it is replaced in a warmer area.

A **Write the cause and effect for each sentence.**

1. When the weather is cooler, some plants become dormant.

   Cause: _____

   Effect: _____

2. A dormant plant does not grow as much, therefore you do not need to water it as much either.

   Cause: _____

   Effect: _____

3. If you water the plant too much, then you could drown it!

   Cause: _____

   Effect: _____

4. Some gardeners will put the plant in a cool place *in order to* fool it into becoming dormant.

   Cause: _____

   Effect: _____

5. The plant "thinks" it is time to bloom again once it is replaced in a warmer area.

   Cause: _____

   Effect: _____

B Circle the 8 cause and effect words and phrases in the puzzle. List them at the right. Note: 4 of them are phrases, and 4 are single words.

B	E	C	A	U	S	E	O	F
R	E	E	S	F	C	M	L	S
I	L	Q	A	W	E	T	U	P
N	F	V	R	F	C	H	N	S
O	Y	V	E	L	T	W	U	I
C	A	U	S	E	S	E	G	N
E	S	Z	U	K	C	B	R	C
B	R	P	L	H	A	U	R	E
E	S	O	T	H	A	T	W	S

_____

_____

_____

_____

_____

_____

_____

_____

C Write your own cause and effect paragraph. Use a starter from below or one of your own. Be sure to use words that signal causes and effects.

> It was such a surprise when . . .
> I can't turn in my homework today because . . .
> Our boat overturned when . . .
> As a result of the frog getting in the house . . .

_____

_____

_____

_____

_____

_____

_____

_____

_____

Name _____

Editing Your Work

 Editing your work is an important step in the writing process. Many tests ask you to show what you know about editing.

A Cody wrote a report about an ocean ecosystem. Help him revise and edit his report. Read the report and answer the questions that follow.

Ocean Currents and Ocean Life

1) Did you know that oceans have rivers running through them? 2) They do! 3) The Gulf Stream is a well-known ocean current. 4) A stream of water runs on a permanently fixed course through the rest of the water. 5) One reason is the saltiness in the water. 6) Having more salt makes the water more dense, which can help to make the water stay separate. 7) Differences in temperature also limit the mixing of ocean water. 8) The temperature may be different because the water came from a different part of the world. 9) Another cause of temperature changes is underwater volcanoes that heat water.

1. The hyphen in the word *well-known* makes the verb *known* into what kind of word? _____

2. How is the word *to* used in sentence 6? What other word or words go with it?

   _____

3. List one complex sentence above and write the dependent clause from the sentence. _____

   _____

4. List four examples of a simple sentence. _____

5. Write two words or phrases from the paragraph that signal cause and effect.

   _____

   _____

6. List four prepositional phrases in the paragraph. _____

   _____

Advantage Grammar Grade 6 © 2005 Creative Teaching Press

B **Continue revising and editing Cody's report.**

1) Just as on land, animals in the ocean live mostly in one area of the same temperature. 2) Although they may visit a cooler or warmer area, animals stay mainly in one region. 3) Some sea creatures migrate, and they sometimes use currents to help them get places faster. 4) Currents also can move animals that are not self propelling, such as coral. 5) Still other animals hunt for smaller fish traveling in the stream.

1. What two words in sentence 4 should be hyphenated? _____
   _____

2. What kind of sentence is sentence 3? _____

3. Add hyphens to separate other syllables in this word from sentence 1.
   t e m - p e r a t u r e

4. List all the prepositional phrases from sentence 1. _____
   _____

5. Which sentence has an infinitive verb, and what is it?
   _____

6. Reread sentence 4. Complete this sentence telling the effect of currents moving coral.
   In this way, coral, _____
   _____
   _____

7. List the prepositions from sentence 5.
   _____

8. Two of the following words are incorrect. Write them correctly.
   eleven-year-old   eleven-years-old   midstream   exsailor   prehistoric
   _____

LESSON

24

PLANTS AND
ANIMALS

Take a Test Drive

Fill in the bubble beside the correct answer.

Jen wrote a report about how organisms act. Help her revise and edit her report. Read the report and answer the questions that follow.

Stimulus and Response

1) Any part of an environment that causes an organism to do something is a stimulus. 2) This includes temperature and the amount of water and air in a place. 3) Even the presence of another organism could bring about a response. 4) If there is too much water, a plant may close its leaves so it won't catch as much rain. 5) An animal in too much water will try to get to drier land.

1. Which phrase is an infinitive?
   Ⓐ to get
   Ⓑ to drier land
   Ⓒ too much water
   Ⓓ none of the above

2. Which phrase is **not** a prepositional phrase?
   Ⓕ to drier land
   Ⓖ in a place
   Ⓗ of water
   Ⓙ to do

3. Which sentence is a complex sentence?
   Ⓐ sentence 2   Ⓒ sentence 4
   Ⓑ sentence 3   Ⓓ sentence 5

4. Which word is **not** correctly broken into syllables?
   Ⓕ this   Ⓗ an-i-mal
   Ⓖ pa-rt   Ⓙ en-vi-ron-ment

5. Which word or phrase does **not** signal a cause or effect?
   Ⓐ so   Ⓒ bring about
   Ⓑ causes   Ⓓ none of the above

Continue revising and editing Jen's report.

1) An organism can also respond to a stimulus within itself. 2) For example, when an animal runs out of energy, it will probably want to eat or sleep. 3) Also, if an animal gets too hot, it may start to sweat to cool itself down. 4) A too-hot plant has its own way of sweating. 5) Just like people, plants could use fans to cool themselves when the temperature is over one-hundred-twenty-five degrees. 6) Otherwise, they could die.

6. Which spelling is correct?
  Ⓕ one-hundred-twenty-five
  Ⓖ one hundred twenty five
  Ⓗ one-hundred twenty-five
  Ⓙ one hundred twenty-five

7. What kind of sentence is sentence 4?
  Ⓐ simple
  Ⓑ complex
  Ⓒ compound
  Ⓓ none of the above

8. Which sentence about the paragraph is completely correct?
  Ⓕ One might say that many organisms are self cooling.
  Ⓖ One might say that many organisms are self-cooling.
  Ⓗ One might say that many organisms are selfcooling.
  Ⓙ none of the above

9. Which phrase is a prepositional phrase?
  Ⓐ to a stimulus
  Ⓑ too hot
  Ⓒ to cool
  Ⓓ to eat

10. Which word or phrase does **not** signal a cause or effect?
  Ⓕ if
  Ⓖ when
  Ⓗ just like
  Ⓙ none of the above

LESSON

25

OUR SOLAR
SYSTEM

Recognizing the Progressive Tense

⭐ A **progressive verb** shows continuing action. It includes a verb and a helping verb.

For years, Neptune **was revolving** in the furthest path from the sun.

Only verbs that show things that can change are progressive verbs.

Not correct: Mercury is being grey.

Progressive verbs can show a process in the past, present, or future.

Past progressive: We **were looking** through our telescope during the eclipse.
Present progressive: I **am thinking** about getting a bigger telescope.
Future progressive: My family **will be saving** up to get it soon.

A Write *Past* if the verb is past progressive, *Present* if it is present progressive, and *Future* if it is future progressive. Underline the progressive verb and any helping verbs.

_____ **1.** A man was making eyeglasses when he began playing with his lenses.

_____ **2.** Many were experimenting with it by the time the glasses maker won an award for his telescope.

_____ **3.** My family is planning a trip to a planetarium with a huge telescope.

_____ **4.** We will be going sometime next month.

_____ **5.** I am learning everything I can about the history of the telescope.

_____ **6.** In fact I will be making a presentation in class about my trip.

_____ **7.** I was looking through my telescope when I saw a shooting star.

_____ **8.** I am trying not to get too excited about our trip.

_____ **9.** My sister is driving my mom crazy asking questions about the trip.

_____ **10.** She and I will be racing each other to get to the big telescope first.

 Advantage Grammar Grade 6 © 2005 Creative Teaching Press

B Write a sentence describing what progressive verbs have in common.

_____

_____

_____

C Write a sentence using the given word.

1. past progressive of *fly*

_____

_____

2. present progressive of *fly*

_____

_____

3. future progressive of *fly*

_____

_____

4. past progressive of *look*

_____

_____

5. present progressive of *look*

_____

_____

6. future progressive of *look*

_____

_____

26

OUR SOLAR
SYSTEM

Using Comparatives and Superlatives

⭐ Add the ending *–er* to most words when comparing two things.

Venus is **closer** to the sun than Earth is.

Its cloud cover is **heavier** than Earth's.

Add *–est* to most words when comparing more than two things.

Mercury is the **closest** planet to the sun

Mercury is **smaller** than Venus.

For longer words, add *more* or *most* instead.

Venus is **more brilliant** than Mars or Saturn.

Venus is the **most brilliant** planet appearing in Earth's sky.

A **Circle the correct word or words to complete the sentence.**

1. Earth is   magneticer   more magnetic   than Venus.

2. Jupiter is the   biggest   most big   planet in our solar system.

3. The rotation of Venus is   slower   more slow   than Earth's.

4. The seasons on Uranus last   longer   more long   than on Earth.

5. Earth is the   densest   most dense   planet in our system.

6. Saturn's rings are   thinner   more thin   thinnest   most thin

   than Jupiter's.

7. Pluto is the   tinyest   tiniest   most tiny   planet.

8. Neptune's orbit is the   more unusual   unusualest   most unusual   of all.

9. Mercury's temperatures are   extremer   more extreme   extremest

   most extreme   than any other plane's.

10. Mars has   interestinger   more interesting   interestingest

   most interesting   land features than most.

B Some comparing words have irregular forms. Complete the chart.

1.	good	better	
2.	bad		worst
3.	little	less	
4.		further	furthest
5.	much		most

C Write three sentences comparing two or more things.

_____

_____

_____

_____

_____

_____

_____

_____

_____

_____

_____

_____

_____

_____

_____

_____

Active and Passive Voice

27

OUR SOLAR
SYSTEM

⭐ When using the **active voice**, the subject is a "do-er."

> Mars contains huge craters created by meteors.
> (Mars does what? It contains craters.)

When using the **passive voice**, the subject is having something done to it.
It is a "be-er."

> Mars has been the subject of many science and science fiction books.
> (Mars doesn't do anything here.)

Sometimes, the actual thing doing the action in a passive sentence is not stated.
You may be able to add an active subject when rewriting the sentence in the
active voice.

> **passive voice:** The gravity of Mars has been found to be one-third
> that of Earth.

> **active voice:** Instruments have found that the gravity of Mars is
> one-third that of Earth.

A **Write A if the sentence is active, write P if it is passive.**

1. _____ a) No water has been found on the planet Mars.

   _____ b) No water exists on the surface of Mars.

2. _____ a) No humans have visited Mars yet.

   _____ b) Mars has not been visited by humans.

3. _____ a) Sometimes Mars is covered by huge dust storms.

   _____ b) Huge dust storms sometimes cover Mars.

4. _____ a) Mars' underground may contain water.

   _____ b) Water may be locked underground on Mars.

B Write *A* if the sentence is active, write *P* if it is passive.

_____ **1.** Mars is so far from the sun, it gets much less sunlight than on Earth.

_____ **2.** Mars has now been visited by several Earth spacecraft.

_____ **3.** The surface of Mars is covered with active volcanoes.

_____ **4.** Mars has almost no oxygen.

C Look at the passive sentences in activities A and B. What are some clues in the sentence that it is passive? What kinds of helping verbs are used with the passive voice?

_____

_____

_____

D Rewrite each passive sentence using the active voice.

1. The largest volcano and the longest canyon in the Solar System can be found on Mars.

_____

_____

_____

2. It is not known if the Mars ice caps are ice made with water.

_____

_____

_____

3. Mars is circled by two moons.

_____

_____

28

OUR SOLAR
SYSTEM

Capitalizing Names and Titles

 Proper names are always capitalized.

> **Dr. Catherine Weitz** was the program scientist for the **Mars Exploration Rover** project.

Capitalize titles only when they are used as a name.

> I think **Mom** knows **Dr. Joy Crisp**, the project scientist.
> My **mom** knows the **doctor** who is the project scientist.

Titles of other things, such as companies and movies, should be capitalized.

> **Paramount** released the movie, **Top Gun**, starring Tom Cruise.

Each letter of an **acronym**, a word in which each letter stands for another word, is capitalized.

> Our school's **PTO** is trying to get an astronaut come speak to us.
> **PTO** stands for Parent-Teacher Organization.

A **Underline the letters that should be capitalized. Remember to capitalize words at the beginning of the sentence as well.**

1. my uncle wanted to be just like john glenn.

2. uncle ray has always admired the famous astronaut.

3. ray is my mom's brother.

4. I was surprised to learn that dad had wanted to be an astronaut too.

5. most astronauts are scientists as well as airplane pilots.

6. doctor david wolf is also a medical doctor!

7. most nasa astronauts are in the military - especially the air force.

8. perhaps astronaut carlos noriega will come speak at glenn school.

Name _____

⭐ The word *earth* is capitalized only when it refers to the planet Earth. The word can also mean the surface of the planet or the soil.

Only one-third of **Earth** has exposed **earth**; the rest is covered by water.

The words *sun* and the *moon* also should not be capitalized unless the sentence also refers to another celestial body (things in the sky).

The **moon** was bright last night.   You could see the **Moon** and the planet **Venus**.

B Complete each sentence with by writing in the correct form of the word in parenthesis.

1. (sun) Try not to look directly at the _____ .

2. (earth) The _____ is too muddy to walk on.

3. (moon) The spacecraft passed the _____ before going to Jupiter.

4. (earth) Would you rather stay here on planet _____ ?

5. (sun) All planets in our system circle around the _____ .

6. (moon) The _____ is closer to us than Mars.

C Write two sentences for each word—one in which the word is capitalized and one in which it is not.

1. mom _____

_____

_____

2. earth _____

_____

_____

Spelling Homophones

L E S S O N

29

OUR SOLAR
SYSTEM

⭐ **Homophones** are words that sound alike but do not mean the same thing, nor are they spelled the same way.

Study the words below.

> there - a certain place
> their - belong to them
> they're - contraction for "they are" or "they were"
>
> its - belong to it
> it's - contraction for "it is"
>
> threw - past tense of throw
> through - in one side and out another
>
> red - the color
> read - past tense of read

A Write the correct word from above in each sentence below.

1. Because of its appearance, Mars is called the _____ planet.

2. I would like to go _____ someday.

3. The rocket went right _____ the Earth's atmosphere.

4. He _____ the binoculars to me.

5. I dropped them, but I don't think _____ broken.

6. Before seeing the move, I _____ as much as I could about

   outer space.

7. I think _____ amazing how much information we already know

   about other planets!

8. I need to go to the Smiths to give them back _____ star chart.

9. Saturn has many rings, the rings are separated by _____

   eighteen moons.

B List other homophones you know.

_____   _____

_____   _____

_____   _____

_____   _____

_____   _____

C Write five sentences using homophones correctly.

_____

_____

_____

_____

_____

_____

_____

_____

_____

_____

_____

_____

LESSON

30

OUR SOLAR
SYSTEM

Compare and Contrast

⭐ When you **compare** things, you tell how they are similar.

Comparison words that connect ideas include:
also, alike, similar to, same, both, likewise, just as, too

When you **contrast** things, you tell how they are different.

Contrast words that connect ideas include:
differ, on the other hand, unlike, however, in contrast to, but

A **Circle words in the paragraph that signal comparisons or contrasts.**

     Saturn and Uranus have many things in common, but also many traits that make them different as well. Both planets are large planets - much larger than Earth. They also both have rings, although Saturn's a bright and Uranus' are dark. From Earth, Saturn looks yellow. But no one on Earth knows yet what color Uranus is. Only space probes from Earth have gone past each of the planets so far.

B **Write the facts about both planets in the overlapping section. Write the facts that make them different in the correct circle.**

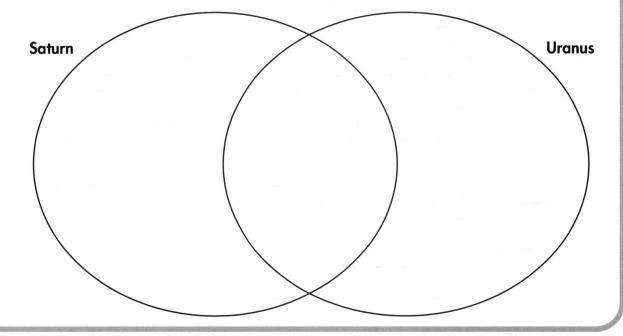

Saturn   Uranus

Advantage Grammar Grade 6 © 2005 Creative Teaching Press

Name _____

Neptune   **Pluto**

is a giant
planet, has at
least three
moons, may
have two rings

at one time or another,
one is always the furthest
planet, both have at least
one moon, it takes a long
time for either of them to
make a complete orbit
around the sun

is a small
planet, scientists
know the least
about this
planet, is known
to have one
moon

C **Use the facts above to write a paragraph comparing and contrasting the planets Neptune and Pluto. Be sure to use words that signal comparisons and contrasts.**

_____

_____

_____

_____

_____

_____

_____

_____

_____

_____

_____

_____

Name _____

Editing Your Work

⭐ Editing your work is an important step in the writing process. Many tests ask you to show what you know about editing.

A Amber wrote a report about locating planets. Help her revise and edit her report. Read Amber's report and follow the directions.

Stars and Planets

1) For centuries, man has been looking up at the stars. 2) Little did early man know that he was also looking at other planets! 3) Five planets can be seen at night without using a telescope. 4) One can see Mercury, Venus, Mars, Jupiter, and Saturn at different times of the night or year. 5) Part of the reason its possible to see a planet on a certain night is because of it's orbit. 6) If it is further out in its orbit around the sun, it may be harder—or even impossible—to see.

1. Which sentence uses the passive voice in the paragraph above? Rewrite it using the active voice. _____

    _____

    _____

2. Rewrite sentence 5, correcting the two mistakes. _____

    _____

    _____

3. Which words in the paragraph are comparing words?

    _____

4. Which sentence has a word that should be capitalized? What is the word?

    _____

5. Which sentence contains a present progressive verb and what is it?

    _____

B **Continue reading and editing Amber's report.**

1) It's difficult; but their are ways to tell the difference between a planet and a star in the night sky. 2) The light reflected from a planet has a more short distance than the light from a star. 3) Because of this, the light is stronger and doesn't twinkle. 4) But it is hard to tell that sometimes. 5) A better way to tell the difference is to watch it over a stretch of time. 6) A planet is most rapid than a star. 7) It will move across the sky much more quickly than the stars, which will keep a pattern. 8) So when you are sitting outside with your Mom or Dad a clear night, try to find a Planet among the Stars.

1. What homophone is used incorrectly in sentence 1? What should the word

   be? _____

2. Rewrite sentence 2 correctly.

   _____

   _____

3. Why is the phrase "most quick" in sentence 6 incorrect? What should the phrase be?

   _____

   _____

4. Rewrite sentence 8 correctly.

   _____

   _____

   _____

5. What are the comparing and contrasting words in the report?

   _____

   _____

6. How are planets and stars different and alike as described by Amber's report?

   Alike: _____

   Different: _____

Take a Test Drive

Fill in the bubble beside the correct answer.

Samuel wrote an essay about meteors. Help him revise and edit his essay. Read Samuel's essay and follow the directions.

1) I was camping with my Dad when we saw a meteor! 2) If you have ever seen a shooting star, then you have seen a meteor, too. 3) I decided then and their that I would read all I could about meteors.

4) Meteors are rocks in space that fall through the Earth's atmosphere. 5) These rocks often come from comets. 6) A comet is a ball of ice and dust. 7) As it approaches the Sun, a comet is slowly being melted by the heat. 8) The dust becomes a meteor. 9) When a comet passes the earth, meteors will shower down. 10) Because scientists know when a comet will be passing by, they can predict a meteor shower.

1. Which phrase uses the passive voice?
   - Ⓐ I was camping
   - Ⓑ you have ever seen
   - Ⓒ rocks often come from comets
   - Ⓓ a comet is slowly being melted

2. Which phrase uses a past progressive verb?
   - Ⓕ was camping
   - Ⓖ have ever seen
   - Ⓗ is being melted
   - Ⓙ will be passing by

3. Which homophone is used incorrectly in the essay?
   - Ⓐ sentence 4 - through
   - Ⓑ sentence 3 - their
   - Ⓒ sentence 3 - read
   - Ⓓ none of the above

4. Which word should **not** be capitalized?
   - Ⓕ sentence 1 - Dad
   - Ⓖ sentence 4 - Earth's
   - Ⓗ sentence 7 - Sun
   - Ⓙ none of the above

Continue reading and editing Samuel's essay.

1) Most meteors are so small, they burn up as they approach Earth. 2) The few that get to the ground are called a "find." 3) They are usually more heavy than a regular rock because it is often iron!

4) Meteors can be seen when the sky is clear and as dark as possible. 5) Next weekend, a meteor shower is scheduled. 6) And dad and I will be camping in the mountains to try to see more shooting stars!

5. Which phrase should be used to correct sentence 3?
   - Ⓐ more heavy
   - Ⓒ heaviest
   - Ⓑ most heavy
   - Ⓓ heavier

6. Which sentence uses the passive voice?
   - Ⓕ sentence 1
   - Ⓗ sentence 5
   - Ⓖ sentence 3
   - Ⓙ sentence 6

7. Which sentence contains a present progressive verb?
   - Ⓐ sentence 2
   - Ⓒ sentence 6
   - Ⓑ sentence 4
   - Ⓓ none of the above

8. Which correction should be made in sentence 6?
   - Ⓕ change "will be camping" to "was camping"
   - Ⓖ change "more shooting" to *shootinger*
   - Ⓗ capitalize the word dad
   - Ⓙ none of the above

9. Which word shows a comparison or contrast?
   - Ⓐ as
   - Ⓒ often
   - Ⓑ more
   - Ⓓ possible

10. Which kind of phrase is used in sentence 4?
   - Ⓕ future progressive verb
   - Ⓖ contrasting words
   - Ⓗ passive voice
   - Ⓙ homophones

Name _____

Adjectives and Adverbs

⭐ An **adjective** describes a noun.

> **fascinating** book   **two red** chairs   **bright reading** light

An **adverb** describes a verb, an adjective, or another adverb.

> read **quickly**   **very** interesting   **quite simply**

A Circle the describing word, draw an arrow from it to the word it describes. Then write *Adj* for adjectives and *Adv* for adverbs. Some sentences will have more than one describing word.

_____ **1.** Shel Silverstein writes funny poems.

_____ **2.** In fact, some say that he is outrageously funny.

_____ **3.** The poet says that we have golden tales to spin.

_____ **4.** He asks if you would like to buy some magic beans.

_____ **5.** The daring acrobats swing on a high-up trapeze.

_____ **6.** Susy secretly spied on an elf.

_____ **7.** The boat sank swiftly and suddenly.

_____ **8.** The children were quite soggy.

⭐ Adjectives also tell number, origin, and qualities.

some **Virginia** ham   those **basketball** players

Adverbs tell condition, placement, frequency, and time.

not walking   sitting **nearby**   leaving **soon**

B Use adjectives and adverbs to write descriptive sentences to answer the question.

1. Where is your room? _____

2. How do you get to school? _____

3. What kind of a reader are you? _____

4. What do you do on vacation? _____

5. How would like to travel? _____

6. What kind of cake do you like? _____

7. How do you cook? _____

8. How do you sleep at night? _____

C Choose one answer from above and add to your description.

_____

_____

_____

_____

_____

_____

_____

Name _____

Subject-Predicate Agreement

⭐ The form of the verb in the predicate should match that of the subject. But be careful. It is easy to confuse nouns in sentences with prepositional phrases.

> correct: The **witch** in the stories **is** not scary at first.
> incorrect: The **witch** in the stories **are** not scary at first.

Witch is the subject; it is singular. *Stories* is the object of the preposition *in*; it is plural. The verb, *is,* is singular. It matches *witch,* the subject.

A Underline the subject of the sentence. Write *S* if the subject is singular and *P* if the subject is plural. Circle the predicate.

_____ **1.** This book by C.S. Lewis is just the first in the series.

_____ **2.** Two brothers and two sisters discover a new world in a piece of furniture.

_____ **3.** The lion in the books is more than just a lion.

_____ **4.** In fact, many animals in Narnia talk and think for themselves.

_____ **5.** Even the trees in the forest are thinking beings.

B Circle the predicate that agrees with the subject.

1. The children   become   becomes   separated.

2. The faun with the umbrella   greet   greets   Lucy kindly.

3. The yard with the statues   seem   seems   creepy.

4. The witch and her servants   love   loves   winter.

5. The giants by the wall   was   were   gentle.

6. The army of good creatures   welcome   welcomes   the children gladly.

7. The box of candies   do   does   tempt Edmund.

8. The beavers in the big dam   explain   explains   the land of Narnia.

Name _____

 Any title is considered a singlar noun, even if it has plural words in it. It takes the singular form of the verb.

The Lion, the Witch and the Wardrobe **tells** about an exciting adventure.

C **Write the correct form of the predicate given.**

1. (be) The chapter "What Happened about the Statues" _____ the best part.

2. (be) Lucy and the faun _____ my favorite characters.

3. (want) Several movie studios in Hollywood _____ to film a movie version.

4. (enjoy) My sister and I _____ reading the book before seeing the movie.

5. (read) Nobody in the family but us _____ the book first.

6. (be) The movie Holes _____ based on a book.

7. (tell) _Harriet Tubman and the Underground Railroad_ _____ a true story.

8. (contain) _Where the Sidewalk Ends_ _____ many poems.

9. (like) The author Shel Silverstein also _____ to sing.

10. (retell) _The Summer of the Swans_ _____ the story of "The Ugly Duckling."

Name _____

Improving Sentences

⭐ You can sometimes improve a sentence by using the active voice rather than the passive vioce.

The book *The Island of the Blue Dolphins* was written by famous author Scott O'Dell.

Better: Famous author Scott O'Dell wrote the book *The Island of the Blue Dolphins.*

But sometimes, changing the voice from passive to active doesn't make sense.

The book was written about a true story.

The sentence could be changed to read: *O'Dell wrote the book about a true story.* But this takes the emphasis off of the fact that the story is true.

A **Rewrite the sentence using the active voice.**

1. Karana was clothed in furs and feathers.

_____

_____

2. Little Ramos was killed by wolves.

_____

_____

3. More historical fiction novels were penned by O'Dell.

_____

_____

_____

4. The Newberry Medal can be added to O'Dell's awards for writing this book.

_____

_____

_____

Name _____

C Rewrite the sentence getting rid of unnecessary words.

1. There are many other good books that were written by Scott O'Dell.

    _____

    _____

2. As a matter of fact, one book was written by him that is about my area of the country where I live.

    _____

    _____

3. People who were living in the area were afraid due to the fact that they thought there was a curse.

    _____

    _____

4. The book *The Black Pearl* concerns people who collect pearls by means of underwater diving.

    _____

    _____

5. All things considered, this book may be the best book about our area that exists.

    _____

    _____

6. For the most part, the book could have been written about someone my grandfather knew.

    _____

    _____

36

LITERATURE

Punctuating Titles

⭐ Titles of long works are put in italics or underlined. These include the titles of novels, movies, albums, works of art, newspapers, magazines, ships, and planes.

My favorite book this year is *The Phantom Tollbooth* by Norton Juster. The movie version uses Mel Blanc, who also did <u>The Bugs Bunny Movie</u>.

Titles of shorter works are put in quotation marks. These works include titles of songs, chapters, articles, short poems, and short stories.

The story "Rikki-Tikki-Tavi" is part of *The Jungle Book*.

Quotation marks go outside commas and periods.

The movie has a great song called, "The Bare Necessities."

 A **Add underlines or quotation marks. (Hint: some sentences may have more than one title in it and others may have none.)**

1. I like the book called From the Mixed-up Files of Mrs. Basil E. Frankweiler.

2. Claudia becomes entranced by the statue Angel.

3. The children hid in the Metropolitan Museum of Art.

4. New York has three major newspapers: The Wall Street Journal, New York Times and Daily News.

5. One article recently was The greatest movie ever.

6. I think the greatest movie is still Shrek.

7. The song from it, Hallelujah, is very pretty.

8. A good chapter in the book Loser is named Win.

9. The funniest section in the magazine Reader's Digest is called Humor in Uniform.

10. I read about Amelia Earhart and her flight in the plane Friendship.

B **Write a complete sentence giving a title to fit the category.**

1. two of your favorite books: _____

_____

2. a chapter in a book:

_____

3. your favorite song: _____

_____

4. the title of a CD:

_____

5. the name of a ship:

_____

6. the name of a newspaper:

_____

7. the names of two magazines: _____

_____

8. the title of a magazine or newspaper article:

_____

9. the name of your favorite movie: _____

_____

10. the name of a short story or poem:

_____

C **Write a few sentences about your favorite book or CD. Give the title and a short description. Then tell your favorite chapter or song and tell why it is your favorite.**

_____

_____

_____

_____

_____

Name _____

Spelling the Schwa Sound

 The **schwa sound** is heard in unaccented syllables and one-syllable words which are considered to have no stress.

The schwa sound can be spelled many different ways.

char`- i - ty     a - dult`   sol` - əmn

The symbol for the schwa sound used in dictionaries and glossary pronunciation guides is ə.

char` ə ty     ə dult`   sol` əmn

A Place a hyphen between syllables. Write an accent symbol after the accented syllable. Then, write the e symbol over the unaccented vowel, or the least accented vowel.

1. lesson
2. instant
3. alone
4. autumn
5. relative

6. contain
7. biscuit
8. minimum
9. magnet
10. sofa

B Circle the words with the schwa sound.

1. star
2. final
3. father
4. label
5. hurry

6. palm
7. fossil
8. keeper
9. score
10. person

C List words from page 76 and other words you know that fit each category.

schwa sound spelled with an a

_____

_____

_____

_____

_____

schwa sound spelled with an o

_____

_____

_____

_____

schwa sound spelled with an e

_____

_____

_____

_____

schwa sound spelled with a u

_____

_____

_____

_____

schwa sound spelled with an i

_____

_____

_____

_____

Name _____

Ordering by Importance

⭐ One way to order sentences in a paragraph is to put the most important points first. Then put the next most important sentence, and so on.

Ordering sentence by importance is especially useful when writing a persuasive paragraph to convince your audience of a point.

1. Write a topic sentence stating your main idea.
2. Write the best point first. Give specific examples, if possible.
3. Write the second best point.
4. Write the third best point, and so on.
5. Consider using a closing sentence, restating the main idea.

The Phantom Tollbooth by Norman Juster is one of the greatest ever books written. First of all, it is interesting on many levels. When Milo visits the Doldrums, for example, it is an actual place, but it also represents the state that he usually lives in (bored). All the silly plays on words also make the book lots of fun. One instance is the confusion over the name of the woman living in the dungeon (she is a which, which also sounds like witch). Finally, the story is a wonderful adventure, full of friends, fun, danger, and plot twists. All these things make the book one everyone should read!

A **Write the points made in the paragraph above in the correct place.**

1. Topic sentence: _____

_____

2. Best point: _____

_____

3. Second best point: _____

_____

4. Third best point: _____

_____

5. Restatement of the topic sentence: _____

_____

     Advantage Grammar Grade 6 © 2005 Creative Teaching Press

⭐ Another way to use order of importance is to build up to the most important point. It is in the exact reverse order of the other order-of-importance paragraph.

B Use the points listed to write a paragraph in reverse order of importance.

_____

_____

_____

_____

_____

_____

_____

_____

_____

_____

_____

_____

_____

_____

_____

_____

Name _____

L E S S O N

39

LITERATURE

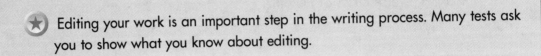

Editing Your Work

⭐ Editing your work is an important step in the writing process. Many tests ask you to show what you know about editing.

A Juan wrote a book report. Help him revise and edit his report. Read the report and answer the questions that follow.

Report on A Wrinkle in Time

1) A Wrinkle in Time by Madeleine L'Engle is a surprisingly good book. 2) Books with a girl main character doesn't always interest me. 3) But this book was great! 4) That's probably due to the fact that I enjoy science fiction stories. 5) This book is all about time travel and space travel. 6) Also, the family in the book seemed like they could be real (even though some of the things that happened to them could not). 7) So their actions were realistic. 8) Finally, I was entertained by the interesting characters, such as Mrs. Who and Mrs. Whatsit.

1. Punctuate titles correctly throughout the report.

2. Which two sentences are in the passive voice? _____

3. Rewrite sentence 2 correctly.

_____

_____

4. List at least eight adjectives from the paragraph. _____

_____

5. How is the paragraph organized? _____

6. List each point.

Best point: _____

_____

Second best point: _____

_____

Third best point: _____

_____

B **Continue revising and editing Juan's report.**

1) The book centers around Meg, a teenage girl. 2) Her father is missing. 3) She meets some very weird ladies who want to help find her father. 4) She, her quirky brother, and a guy from her school travels through time and space with the ladies. 5) They actually find her father in chapter 8, The Transparent Column. 6) However, there are still four chapters to go! 7) I don't want to spoil it for you if you want to read A Wrinkle in Time; so I'll stop now!

1. Punctuate titles correctly throughout the report.

2. What should be changed in sentence 4 and why? _____
   _____

3. Rewrite sentence 6 leaving out the words "there are." _____
   _____

4. List the four adverbs and the words they describe.
   _____
   _____
   _____

5. List the five adjectives and the words they describe.
   _____
   _____
   _____

6. Place a hyphen between the syllables, add an accent after the accented syllable, and write e over the vowel that makes the schwa sound.

   1. c e n t e r s   4. t r a v e l s

   2. a r o u n d   5. t r a n s p a r e n t

   3. f a t h e r   6. c o l u m n

LESSON

40

LITERATURE

Take a Test Drive

Fill in the bubble beside the correct answer.

Christina wrote a book report. Help her revise and edit her report. Read the report and answer the questions that follow.

"Artemis Fowl" Book Report

1) *Artemis Fowl* by Eoin Colfer is a very strange and wonderful adventure.
2) It is strange because it mixes fairies with high-tech stuff and modern-day criminals.
3) And it's wonderful because it's fun and surprising. 4) One thing that surprised me was that the fairies' way of life included budgets and deadlines—like in the real world.
5) Another good part is that you get to be part of the adventure in that, if you crack the code in the margins of the book, you'll get some inside information that isn't revealed anywhere else. 6) The best part was that it was comedy, science-fiction, mystery, and adventure all rolled into one! 7) If you like any of those kind of books, you should read this one!

1. Which is the most important point about the book?
  Ⓐ It's strange.
  Ⓑ It's surprising.
  Ⓒ It fits several categories of books.
  Ⓓ If you crack the code, you get more information.

2. Which is **not** the correct way to write the title of the book?
  Ⓕ Artemis Fowl
  Ⓗ "Artemis Fowl"
  Ⓖ *Artemis Fowl*
  Ⓙ none of the above

3. Which sentence is too wordy and should be rewritten?
  Ⓐ sentence 2
  Ⓑ sentence 5
  Ⓒ sentence 6
  Ⓓ sentence 7

4. Which word is **not** an adjective?
  Ⓕ modern-day
  Ⓗ strange
  Ⓖ wonderful
  Ⓙ very

Advantage Grammar Grade 6 © 2005 Creative Teaching Press

Continue revising and editing Christina's report.

1) <u>Artemis Fowl</u> begins where we meet Artemis. 2) He's the main character even though he's kind of the bad guy! 3) Although he's only twelve, he is very smart, has lots of money, and has his own servant. 4) He wants to prove to the world that fairies exist. 5) He also wants to get rich by doing it, too. 6) So he kidnaps Holly Short, a captain with the fairy police. 7) Of course, the fairies back home wants their officer back, not to mention the fact that they don't want people to know about them. 8) You'll have to read the book to find out what happens!

5. What change should be made to sentence 1?
   Ⓐ The title of the book should be in quotes.
   Ⓑ The word "begins" should be "begin."
   Ⓒ both of the above
   Ⓓ none of the above

6. Which word does **not** have the schwa sound?
   Ⓕ people   Ⓗ happen
   Ⓖ world   Ⓙ servant

7. Which word is an adverb?
   Ⓐ bad   Ⓒ main
   Ⓑ back   Ⓓ smart

8. What change should be made to sentence 7?
   Ⓕ Delete the words "the fact that."
   Ⓖ The word "wants" should be "want."
   Ⓗ both of the above
   Ⓙ none of the above

Direct and Indirect Objects

41

JUST FOR FUN

⭐ Since the subject is generally the do-er in the sentence, the **direct object** is the receiver.

I gave away **my card collection**.   Now I want **it** back.

The indirect object is the who or what the action is for or to.

I gave **my brother** the best card.   I actually sold **him** my favorite.
      indirect object   direct object   indirect object   direct object

Some object pronouns are different from subject pronouns.

Subject pronouns: I, we, you, he, she, it, they
Object pronouns: me, us, you, him, her, it, them

A **Write *DO* if the italicized words are the direct object. Write *ID* if they are the indirect object.**

_____ **1.** He threw *the ball* at the last minute.

_____ **2.** The center threw *me* the ball.

_____ **3.** The ref told *me* to stop.

_____ **4.** I did a *free shot*.

_____ **5.** You can send *your fan mail* now.

_____ **6.** I sent *the coach* a card.

_____ **7.** Mom baked *us* a cake.

_____ **8.** My folks named *my brother Julius* after their favorite basketball player.

_____ **9.** I sent you *an E-mail* last night.

_____ **10.** Did you send *me* a reply?

    Advantage Grammar Grade 6 © 2005 Creative Teaching Press

B Write a few words telling how to find the direct and indirect objects in a sentence.

_____

_____

_____

C Circle the subject, underline the direct object, and draw a box around the indirect object. (Remember: every sentence has a subject, but not necessarily an object.)

1. I bought myself new trading cards.

2. My friends and I trade them.

3. We give each other presents of them.

4. Our hobby is fun and entertaining.

5. Mom doesn't understand us.

6. She gives the club cookies and lemonade anyway.

D Circle the pronoun that correctly completes the sentence.

1. Mom got   I   me   a treat.

2. She   Her   always makes my birthday special.

3. Mom brought   we   us   to the basketball court early.

4. We   Us   thought we'd see the team warm-up.

5. Some team members were already on the court; but   they   them   came to us!

6. We were so excited to meet   they   them!

LESSON

Appositives

42

JUST FOR FUN

⭐ An appositive is a re-naming of a noun.

I need to play my favorite instrument, the piano, for someone besides myself.

An appositive can also further explain a noun.

The weirdest group of musicians in school, the jazz band, welcomed me into their group.

An appositive can be one word or many.

The director Mr. Johnson let me try out.

A **Draw a line from the appositive to the noun it renames or explains.**

1. I sit by Kathleen, the bass player.

2. I learned to comp, or accompany, a solo.

3. Mostly seventh- and eighth-graders, the other members are a strange mix.

4. The drummer plays in The Fresh Men, a high school rock band.

5. One sax, that is, a saxophone player, is on the football team.

6. A trumpet taught me to improv, or make up my own solo on the spot.

7. The 'bones (the trombone section) are forming their own hip-hop group.

8. We went to hear my new favorite musician, Joshua Redman, a sax player.

 Advantage Grammar Grade 6 © 2005 Creative Teaching Press

B What clues or signals helped you find the appositives?

_____

_____

_____

C Write six sentences using appositives. Use the examples in the box or create your own.

my teacher	sports idol	the best movie of all time
popular singer	usually done outdoors	
	my favorite restaurant	

_____

_____

_____

_____

_____

_____

_____

_____

_____

_____

_____

_____

_____

43

JUST FOR FUN

Forming Negative Sentences

 Words that make a sentence negative are **negative adverbs**.

no   not   seldom   rarely   hardly   never   few   little

Many contractions are a combination of a helping verb with a negative adverb.

don't=do + not   isn't=is + not   won't=will + not

A **Study the pattern of negative sentences. Describe the pattern using parts of speech. The first one is done for you.**

1. It will not work. _subject, helping verb, negative adverb, predicate_

2. My dog will not sit. _____

3. Can't you come for dinner? _____

4. Aren't you cooking tonight? _____

B **Use the patterns above to answer the questions.**

1. Where does a negative adverb usually come in a statement?

   _____

2. What is different about the pattern for questions?

   _____

C **Complete the sentence with a negative adverb.**

1. I _____ want to practice today.

2. In fact, I _____ want to practice, although I know it helps me.

3. _____ we invent a way to improve without practicing?

4. It seems like the star player _____ ever practices.

5. _____ we want to become a star player, too?

Advantage Grammar Grade 6 © 2005 Creative Teaching Press

⭐ Another way to make a sentence negative is to use a negative prefix.

un-   in-   dis-   non-   anti-

D Circle the negative word in the sentence. Write your own definition for the word. The first one is done for you.

1. My pet rock is (inactive). _not active_____

2. A shot in the arm may not hurt, but it will cause discomfort. _____

3. My grandma seems to go nonstop! _____

4. I was uninformed before I got your note. _____

5. The school has a new antipollution motto. _____

E Write two of your own negative sentences using words you found in the word search above.

_____

_____

_____

_____

_____

_____

_____

_____

_____

_____

_____

Name _____

⭐ Use parentheses ( ) to indicate words in your sentence that are not part of the main thought. Punctuation goes outside the parentheses.

Everyone in my family has gone white-water rafting before—except me (and the dog).

Parentheses can indicate a further explanation, such as an appositive.

We're planning a rafting trip that starts in Ohiopyle (in Pennsylvania).

A **Look at the words in parentheses. Write *NMI* for "not the main idea" or *FE* for "further explanation."**

_____ 1. I have gone canoeing before (when I was a Scout).

_____ 2. Dad (our expert boater) thinks I'm ready for rafting.

_____ 3. Rafts are better for whitewater than a canoe (or kayak).

_____ 4. White water is rapids that churn the water faster (surf also is white water).

_____ 5. White water is faster, so it's more fun - and more dangerous (but that's okay).

_____ 6. Our home (in West Virginia) is close to several big rivers.

B **Add ending parenthesis to the sentence.**

1. To raft on the Potomac River, you must be at least 8 years old (my sister is 9 .

2. We want to raft on the Potomac (the Barnum Whitewater Area .

3. We heard this is the best trip (the North Branch is supposed to be the nicest trip .

4. Ray (Aunt Kristin's boyfriend wants to come with us on our trip.

5. They (the rafting guides give a short training session before we start.

Name _____

 Also use parentheses to add a reference.

Rivers and streams have been liquid highways for years (*The Complete Whitewater Rafter*, p. 1).

The river...had a new story to tell every day (Mark Twain).

Parentheses can also set apart numbers or letters indicating a list.

To go rafting you must wear 1) a life jacket, 2) a helmet, and 3) clothes you can get wet!

Most rafters should avoid (a) waterfalls, (b) low water, and (c) unusually high water.

C **Add parentheses to the sentence.**

1. This river has three classes 1 easiest, 2 slow and fast areas, and 3 more advanced.

2. Serious rafters should read *River Rescue: A Manual for Safety* by S. Ray.

3. The surest road to inspiration is preparation Lloyd George.

4. Trick moves are described in the book *Playboating* by Eric Jackson chapter 1.

5. If you compete in a water rodeo, you should do these trick moves: 1 surf, 2 kickflip, 3 spin, 4 loop, or 5 a wavewheel.

D **Add parentheses to the sentence.**

1. Rafters in the west should read *River Runners' Guide to Utah* the author is Thomas Rampton.

2. A story is worth a thousand pictures Ingram .

3. I would like to raft on 1 the Snake River and 2 the Grand Canyon.

4. The Grand Canyon has a river running through it the Colorado .

5. You can also hike into the canyon or just look from above it .

Name _____

Spelling Commonly Misspelled Words

 Learn the difference between these commonly misspelled homophones.

dessert - a dish served at the end of a meal

desert - a very dry area, to abandon

past - an earlier time

passed - past tense of pass

weather - conditions such as temperature and rain or snow

whether - if

very -extremely

vary - to change

Some words are only confused in certain circumstances.

of - coming from, caused by, about

have - helping verb showing completed action

course - a set or determined action

coarse - rough

 A **Circle the correct word.**

1. If I eat my vegetables, may I have   dessert   desert ?

2. I would like to know   weather   whether   or not we have apples.

3. I think we   past   passed   that car before.

4. Our dog does not like it when we   very   vary   our schedule.

5. Of   course   coarse   we want you to come along too!

6. They should   of   have   gotten here by now!

7. We drove through the   dessert   desert   just to look around.

8. This may have been an ocean floor in the   passed   past.

9. Mom always wants to know about tomorrow's   weather   whether.

10. I do not think highly   of   have   the newscaster.

11. It was raining   very   vary   hard when he said it would sunny.

12. The cat's tongue feels   course   coarse.

⭐ A few words are sometimes compound words - but not all the time. The best way to determine if it is compound is to look at how it is used in the sentence.

may be - a helping verb and verb meaning *could be*
maybe - an adverb meaning *perhaps*

every day - and adjective and noun meaning *each day*
everyday - an adjective meaning *ordinary*

nobody - a pronoun meaning no persons
no body - an adverb and noun meaning *no corpse* or *no collection*

B **Complete the sentences using words from the list above.**

1. She's sad because _____ came to her open house.

2. It _____ that we will get rain today.

3. We will get to see each other _____ .

4. _____ of water exists in this desert.

5. A rainbow is not an _____ occurence!

6. _____ we'll have time for a walk after dinner.

C **Use five homophones or compound words in your own sentences.**

_____

_____

_____

_____

_____

_____

_____

_____

Descriptive Passages

LESSON
46
JUST FOR FUN

★ Adjectives are fine to use in descriptions, but sometimes they aren't as descriptive as they could be.

> Rachel is such a nice person.

Use word pictures and interesting verbs to write better descriptions.

> Rachel's warm smile seems to bring sunshine into any room.

Show how and why things are the way they are. Then, show, don't tell! (What did she *do* that was nice? What does nice look like?)

> Rachel always makes sure to greet new people. She tries to get to know them and help others to, as well.

A **Write a sentence that better describes the scene given. Be creative!**

1. Derek was a good athlete. _____

_____

_____

2. The two were best friends. _____

_____

_____

3. Jessi spends a lot of time outside. _____

_____

_____

4. David really wanted to act in a play. _____

_____

Advantage Grammar Grade 6 © 2005 Creative Teaching Press

⭐ When you write a descriptive paragraph, think of one overall impression you want to give. Describe it in your topic sentence. Add details that support the impression.

Confusing description: The beautiful woods felt creepy.
Are the woods beautiful or creepy? The words don't seem to go together.

Better description: The dark woods close in around you and leave you feeling like you're being watched.

B **Write a descriptive passage. Use an idea from the box or one of your own.**

| My Dad   A Really Bad Day   Families Are Funny |
| An Interesting Show   The Best Thing About Being the Oldest |
| The Best Thing About Being the Youngest |

_____

_____

_____

_____

_____

_____

_____

_____

_____

_____

_____

_____

_____

47

Editing Your Work

Editing your work is an important step in the writing process. Many tests ask you to show what you know about editing.

A Maria wrote an essay about a place. Help her revise and edit her essay. Read the beginning of her essay and answer the questions that follow.

My Favorite Place

1) My favorite place is not a place I get to go to everyday. 2) In fact, I've only been there a few times in the passed. 3) One summer, my parents sent me to Camp Wanakee. 4) Over the hill from the cabins is a small pond with a red barn next to it. 5) The activity director, Dave, sleeps in the hayloft (but he doesn't sleep in hay. 6) I love that place because it is so beautiful. 7) Lots of animals come to the pond. 8) Cattails surround the pond; and you can see the barn reflected in it. 9) When I go there, I feel like I never want to leave.

1. What needs to be corrected in sentence 1?

   _____

2. In which sentence is a parenthesis missing? _____ Write it in the correct place.

3. What is the direct object in sentence 3? _____

4. What needs to be corrected in sentence 2? _____

5. Which sentence has an appositive? Tell what it is and whether it renames or

   further explains something. _____

   _____

6. What are the three negative words in the paragraph?

   _____

7. Rewrite one sentence from the paragraph to make it more descriptive.

   _____

8. What are the two direct objects in sentence 8?

   _____

                    Advantage Grammar Grade 6 © 2005 Creative Teaching Press

Name _____

B **Read the rest of Maria's essay and answer the questions.**

1) One time my tribe (my group of campers) slept in the woods on the hill. 2) In the middle of the night it started to rain. 3) Then a few things happened at once: (a) everybody woke up vary quickly, (b) the counselors shouted for us to go to the barn, and (c we all tried to wriggle out of our sleeping bags and find our shoes. 4) By the time we ran around the pond to the barn, we were all very wet! 5) We laughed at the funny situation, then settled back in to try to sleep again. 6) The rain on the roof put us to sleep right away. 7) When we woke up, Dave was already making us breakfast! 8) It ended up being a great adventure!

1. Which word in sentence 3 is an incorrect homophone? What word should it be?

   _____

2. In which sentence is a parenthesis missing? _____ Write it in the correct place.

3. What is the direct object in sentence 7?

   _____

4. What is the indirect object in sentence 7?

   _____

5. Which sentence uses parentheses around an appositive? What does it rename?

   _____

6. Rewrite one sentence making it negative.

   _____

   _____

7. Rewrite one sentence from the paragraph to make it more descriptive.

   _____

   _____

   _____

Name _____

Take a Test Drive

Fill in the bubble beside the correct answer.

Christian wrote an essay about a summer experience. Help him revise and edit his essay. Read the essay and answer the questions that follow.

The Tallest Slide in the World

1) Last summer I went to Dover Water Park with my cousins, Evan and Alexa. 2) They live so close they can go anytime they want. 3) The first thing we saw when we got into the park is the whitewater rapids that we'd have to take a chairlift to get to the top! 4) But right in the middle of the park is an even taller slide, the Speed Slide. 5) Of coarse, that was what my cousins wanted to go on first! 6) I didn't want them to dessert me; so I had to act brave and go on it, too.

1. Which phrase is an appositive?
   Ⓐ Evan and Alexa
   Ⓑ the Speed Slide
   Ⓒ both of the above
   Ⓓ none of the above

2. Which homophone is used correctly in the paragraph?
   Ⓕ coarse   Ⓗ both of the above
   Ⓖ dessert   Ⓙ none of the above

3. What needs to be corrected in sentence 2?
   Ⓐ the words *so close* should be in parentheses
   Ⓑ the word *anytime* should be two words: *any time*
   Ⓒ both of the above
   Ⓓ none of the above

4. Which best describes the word *me* in sentence 6?
   Ⓕ an appositive
   Ⓖ a negative word
   Ⓗ the direct object
   Ⓙ the indirect object

Continue editing and revising Christian's essay.

1) A boy handed us each a mat at the bottom of the slide. 2) After climbing eight flights of stairs, we were the highest people in the county! 3) I could see the entire park and the road outside the park (but I didn't look). 4) Evan went down the slide first. 5) He looked so small at the bottom, I could barely tell it was him. 6) I wondered if it wouldn't be easier to go back down the stairs. 7) But Alexa looked at me. 8) So I sat down on my mat and closed my eyes. 9) When I got to the bottom, I realized how fun it could of been. 10) If my cousins ask me to go again, we'll start at the Speed Slide again (I think).

5. Which best describes the word *us* in sentence 1?
   Ⓐ an appositive
   Ⓑ a negative word
   Ⓒ the direct object
   Ⓓ the indirect object

6. Which is the best descriptive sentence to replace sentence 7?
   Ⓕ But Alexa smiled.
   Ⓖ But Alexa was staring at me.
   Ⓗ But Alexa was looking at me.
   Ⓙ But Alexa had an expectant look on her face.

7. Which is word is **not** a negative word?
   Ⓐ but   Ⓒ barely
   Ⓑ didn't   Ⓓ wouldn't

8. What needs to be corrected in sentence 9?
   Ⓕ the words *When I got to the bottom* should be in parentheses
   Ⓖ the word *fun* should be *unfun*
   Ⓗ the word *of* should be *have*
   Ⓙ *it* should have a referent

9. Why are the words *but I didn't look* in parentheses in sentence 10?
   Ⓐ It's a further explanation.
   Ⓑ It's not the main idea.
   Ⓒ It renames the park.
   Ⓓ none of the above

Practice Test

Aaron wrote an essay about a sport he enjoys. Help him revise and edit his essay. Read his essay and answer the questions that follow.

Racquetball

1) I have been playing tennis for almost three years now. 2) My friend Ben introduced me to a new game (at least it's new to me). 3) Unlike tennis, racquetball must be played indoors. 4) This is because the court uses four walls and the ceiling. 5) With racquetball, you can bounce the ball off anything, but with tennis, that would be out of bounds. 6) The biggest difference in the courts is that there is no net in racquetball. 7) The racquet used in racquetball looks a lot like a tennis racquet, but it is not like the shape and feel. 8) The racquetball ball is very different from a tennis ball—it is smaller and bouncyer. 9) Despite the differences, racquetball and tennis are both fun games.

1. Which phrase contains an appositive?
   - Ⓐ My friend Ben
   - Ⓑ With racquetball
   - Ⓒ (at least it's new to me)
   - Ⓓ different in shape and feel

2. Which word should be changed in sentence 8?
   - Ⓕ *very* should be *vary*
   - Ⓖ *smaller* should be *smallest*
   - Ⓗ *bouncyer* should be *bouncier*
   - Ⓙ *smaller* should be "more small"

3. Which word from sentence 3 is the main verb?
   - Ⓐ be   Ⓒ unlike
   - Ⓑ must   Ⓓ played

4. Which sentence is a compound sentence?
   - Ⓕ Sentence 3
   - Ⓖ Sentence 5
   - Ⓗ Sentence 6
   - Ⓙ Sentence 9

Answer the questions.

5. Which phrase is an infinitive verb?
   - Ⓐ to me
   - Ⓑ to follow
   - Ⓒ is playing
   - Ⓓ had been trying

6. Which is the correct way to punctuate a song title?
   - Ⓕ *Do You Know*
   - Ⓖ Do You Know
   - Ⓗ 'Do You Know'
   - Ⓙ "Do You Know"

7. What kind of word does the adverb in italics describe? It feels *too* cold to swim today.
   - Ⓐ verb
   - Ⓑ noun
   - Ⓒ adverb
   - Ⓓ adjective

8. Which list is in alphabetical order?
   - Ⓕ shiny, spiny, stinky, spiky
   - Ⓖ shiny, spiky, spiny, stinky
   - Ⓗ shiny, spiny, spiky, stinky
   - Ⓙ spiky, spiny, stinky, shiny

9. Which italicized word is **not** used correctly?
   - Ⓐ Wrong numbers are an *everyday* occurrence here.
   - Ⓑ The show-off tried to seem *all-knowing*.
   - Ⓒ He threw the ball *through* the hoop.
   - Ⓓ I could *of* done better than I did.

10. Which is the indirect object in the sentence? She served me lunch.
    - Ⓕ me
    - Ⓖ she
    - Ⓗ lunch
    - Ⓙ served

11. Which is the preposition in the sentence? I want to play in the pool.
    - Ⓐ to
    - Ⓑ in
    - Ⓒ want
    - Ⓓ play

Practice Test

Megan wrote an essay about a game. Help her revise and her essay. Read the beginning of her essay and answer the questions that follow.

A Live Video Game

1) Every Sunday afternoon my family plays a live video game: laser tag. 2) If you like shooting things, you'll like this game! 3) My family and I plays with two other families as well as anyone else there. 4) The first thing you do when you go to play is pick a nickname. 5) I am Maddog Megan (my dad loves that name because he says it is the opposite of my personality). 6) Then you put on your gear. 7) The gear includes a harness you wear and your laser gun (more about these later). 8) The last thing you do before the game starts is to go over the rules with the marshal, the laser tag referee.

12. How is this paragraph structured?
   - Ⓕ Compare and Contrast
   - Ⓖ Chronological Order
   - Ⓗ Order of Importance
   - Ⓙ Cause and Effect

13. What kind of information is in the parentheses in sentence 5?
   - Ⓐ information that is not the main idea
   - Ⓑ further explanation
   - Ⓒ an appositive
   - Ⓐ a reference

14. Which word does **not** have a schwa sound?
   - Ⓕ marshal   Ⓗ laser
   - Ⓖ referee   Ⓙ gear

15. What is the subject in sentence 7?
   - Ⓐ laser gun   Ⓒ gear
   - Ⓑ harness   Ⓓ you

16. What needs to be corrected in sentence 3?
   - Ⓕ *there* should be *their*
   - Ⓖ *plays* should be *play*
   - Ⓗ *there* should be *they're*
   - Ⓙ none of the above

Continue editing and revising Megan's essay.

1) Finally we're allowed into the arena. 2) It is a maze with two levels. 3) There are dead ends, ramps, windows, and mirrors all over to confuse you. 4) It is also dark and smoky. 5) The only lights are black lights and strobe lights. 6) When you go in, your harness turns on, which means that sensors on your shoulders, tummy, and back light up. 7) You use your laser gun to shoot other people's sensors. 8) If you get shot, your gun turns off for five seconds. 9) You get points for hitting others. 10) But of course, points are taken away if you are hit. 11) We walk around trying to tag (shoot) others without getting tagged. 12) It's lots of fun!

17. Which sentence is the best rewrite of sentence 3?
   Ⓐ There are many dead ends, ramps, windows, and mirrors all over due to the fact that they want to confuse you.
   Ⓑ There are dead ends, ramps, windows, and mirrors all over in order to confuse you.
   Ⓒ All over, there is dead ends, ramps, windows, and mirrors to confuse you.
   Ⓓ All over, dead ends, ramps, windows, and mirrors confuse you.

18. Which sentence is complex?
   Ⓕ sentence 3   Ⓗ sentence 7
   Ⓖ sentence 6   Ⓙ sentence 10

19. Which phrase is an independent clause?
   Ⓐ if you get shot
   Ⓑ when you go in
   Ⓒ points are taken away
   Ⓓ to shoot other people's sensors

20. Which sentence is in the passive voice?
   Ⓕ sentence 1   Ⓗ sentence 6
   Ⓖ sentence 3   Ⓙ sentence 8

21. Which is the direct object in sentence 7?
   Ⓐ You
   Ⓑ to shoot
   Ⓒ your laser gun
   Ⓓ other people's sensors

Lesson 1

A
1. is
2. is
3. seems
4. become
5. are
6. tastes
7. seem
8. grows

B
1. she
2. any subject pronoun fits - I, she, he
3. they

C
ordered helping, then main
1. can, be – made
2. have, been – cooking
3. had – found
4. may, have – weighed
5. will – pour
6. Did – experiment
7. would – break
8. might – mix
9. do – start
10. must – review

Lesson 2

A
1. P
2. S
3. P
4. S
5. P
6. S

B
1. does
2. know
3. are
4. breaks
5. makes
6. are

C
Sentences will vary. Type of form to use is given.
1. plural
2. singular
3. singular
4. singular
5. plural
6. singular

D
Sentences will vary.

Lesson 3

A
1. blue
2. sodium
3. powder
4. compound
5. you

B
1. are
2. become
3. lit
4. use
5. fire

C
ordered subject, then predicate
1. someone designs
2. program allows
3. He tell
4. that added
5. factory connects
6. system check
7. It reports
8. Pyrotechnicians start
9. there is
10. displays are
11. you watch
12. they have

Lesson 4

A
The word that should have a colon after it is given:
1. categories:
2. things:
3. says:
4. following:
5. 8:30

B
1. possible:
2. atoms:
3. none
4. none

C
Subject: chemistry workshop
Date: Mon, Sept 6, 2004 9:30

Dear Mrs. Caraway:
I'm looking forward to coming to your classroom Friday to give the chemistry workshop. Am I remembering that I can start setting up after 12:00 and that we start class at 1:15?

Please send me the following items: directions to your school, a list of your class's special interests, and any questions from your students about being a scientist.

If you send the questions by Thursday, I can make an interesting presentation of the answers.

See you soon,
RaeAnn (Ms. Wizard)

Lesson 5

A
1. e
2. d
3. f
4. b

B

Answers may vary. Sample answers given:
1. having to do with history
2. one who makes art
3. skill with teeth

4. one who announces
5. having appeared
6. the state of being an infant

C

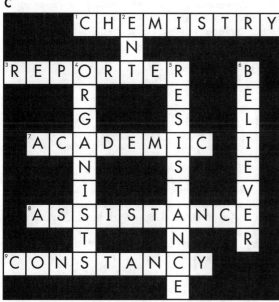

D

Sentences will vary.
1. chemistry – noun
2. ent - suffix
3. reporter – noun
4. organist – noun
5. resistance – noun
6. believer – noun
7. academic – adjective
8. assistance – noun
9. constancy – noun

Lesson 6
A
Answers may vary.
Sometimes, But, For instance, In fact, and

B
Answers will vary. Sample answers given:
Next, Before, Then, Finally

C
words: still, finally, but, besides, next, however, since, second, therefore, soon, last, otherwise, though
message: Transitions are good, but do not use too many!

D
Answers will vary.

Lesson 7
A
1. is made
2. made
3. Electrons, circle
4. relating to atoms
5. relating to magnets
6. sentence 12
7. sentence 3
8. You heard

B
1. it forms
2. Sample answer given: For example, nitrogen, a common gas, has six protons.
3. 3-was, 5-can, 6-might, 7-can
4. skill in chemicals
5. before an explanation
6. A chemist works in lots of places: pharmacies, food companies, or even power companies.
7. Answers may vary: The word one in sentence 3 refers to protons in sentence 2.

Lesson 8
1. D
2. G
3. A
4. F
5. D
6. F
7. D
8. H

Unit 2
Lesson 9
A
1. S
2. P
3. S
4. P
5. P

B
1. sits
2. were
3. are
4. stands
5. are
6. take
7. hang-glide
8. has

C
ordered subject(s), predicate(s)
1. mountains, jut-slope
2. airport, is
3. rains, cause
4. Brazil, is
5. flatland and mountains, house and support

D
1. are
2. houses
3. live
4. root, swim
5. swim
6. comes
7. flies, squawks
8. hunt
9. collect, create
10. are

Answer Key

Lesson 10

A

1. Anyone
2. anybody
3. Someone
4. somebody
5. Nobody
6. One
7. Some
8. Several
9. Few
10. no one
11. neither
12. everything
13. all
14. Something

B

Sentences will vary.

Lesson 11

A

1. IC
2. DC
3. DC

B

1. IC, DC
2. DC, IC
3. IC, DC
4. DC, IC
5. DC, IC

C

1. 1, underline: If you find a place with little artificial light
2. 1
3. 2
4. 1, underline: that the photos of the Lights aren't real.
5. 1
6. 1, underline: that we can't see the Lights here often.
7. 1
8. 1

Lesson 12

A

1. Nepal, but
2. kingdom, yet
3. city, and
4. climate, for
5. climate, so

B

1. none
2. none
3. air, so
4. none
5. mountain, and

C

1. adventures; you
2. Elizabeth II; he
3. together; neither

D

Sentences may vary. Sample answers given:
1. Hillary and Norgay found George Mallory's body on their climb, but they couldn't tell if Mallory had reached the summit or not.
2. Norgay had tried many times to reach the summit of Mt. Everest; he probably spent more time on the mountain than anyone else in history!
3. Tenzing Norgay passed away in 1986; Sir Hillary is still alive.

Lesson 13

A

1. 1, 2
2. 2, 1
3. 3, 2, 1
4. 3, 2, 1, 4
5. 2, 3, 1, 4

B

1. canyon, harbor, mountain, reef, volcano, waterfall
2. Argentina, Armenia, Albania, Angola, Australia, Austria
3. Anguilla, Antigua, Aruba, Bahamas, Barbados, Barbuda, Bermuda
4. Vermont, Virginia, Washington, West Virginia, Wisconsin, Wyoming

C

1. G, J	5. F
2. D, H	6. B
3. E	7. A
4. C	8. I

D

1. 2, 3, 4, 1
2. 1, 4, 2, 3
3. 3, 2, 4, 1
4. 4, 2, 3, 1
5. 1, 2, 3, 4

E

1. Australia, Brazil, Mexico, Nepal, U.S.A., Zambia
2. Grand Canyon, Great Barrier Reef, Harbor of Rio de Janeiro, Mt. Everest, Northern Lights, Paracutin Volcano, Victoria Falls

Lesson 14

A

Paragraphs will vary but should contain order words.

B and C

2, 1, 3, 4

D and E

2, 3, 1

Advantage Grammar Grade 5 © 2005 Creative Teaching Press

Lesson 15
A
1. For weeks, the townspeople had heard what sounded like thunder, but the skies were always clear.
2. sentence 4, a farmer and his wife; sentence 7, ashes, smoke, and rocks
3. Nobody
4. The field and the town were covered in ashes.
5. As they watched,
6. 5, 4, 3, 1, 2

B
1. It does not have a subject or a predicate.
2. Several
3. But now, Paricutin Volcano is safe; it is no longer active.
4. a comma - 1900s, so
5. sentence 10
6. natural, of, seven, the, wonders, world
7. Lists may include: Over the next nine years, one of the last, but now

Lesson 16
1. B
2. H
3. B
4. H
5. B
6. J
7. A
8. G
9. D

Unit 3
Lesson 17
A
1. to keep
2. to decide
3. to survive
4. to continue
5. to be
6. to protect

B
1. e
2. a
3. f
4. c
5. b
6. d

C
1. to find
2. to divide
3. to decide
4. none
5. to use, to examine

D
1. to use, to see
2. to drop
3. to let
4. to squint
5. to keep
6. none

Lesson 18
A
1. on the windowsill
2. in the pot
3. beneath the stairs
4. in front, of a window
5. to a plant, with sunlight, without it
6. during our experiment
7. of the same kind
8. except for the amount, of sunlight

B
the preposition is listed first, then the entire phrase
1. after, after our first experiment
2. of and over, of our plants, over time
3. besides and of, besides our notes, of each pot
4. since, since the beginning

C
1. I, take
2. P, store
3. I, get
4. P, garden
5. P, Mom
6. P, plant
7. I, have
8. I, ask

D
Sentences will vary.

Lesson 19
A
1. Cmpd
2. S
3. S
4. Cmpd
5. Cmpd
6. S

B
Sentences will vary.

C
1. S
2. S
3. Cplx, When an animal creates its own light
4. Cmpd
5. S
6. S
7. Cplx, which helps them hide in darkness
8. Cplx, Although they may never see light themselves,

D
Sentences will vary.

Lesson 20
A
1. forty-six [wol]
2. three-fourths [wol]
3. none
4. none
5. one hundred fifty-six
6. seven-eighths

B
1. hy/phe/nate
2. one-syllable word
3. u/nit
4. sim/ple
5. com/pound
6. or/ga/nism
7. one-syllable word
8. gram/mar
9. sen/tence
10. pa/ra/graphs

C
1. midweek
2. pre-Reagan
3. self-taught
4. prehistoric
5. mid-March
6. ex-wife
7. post-Canadian
8. midday
9. self-seeking
10. ex-president
11. all-inclusive
12. non-British

Answer Key

D
Answers will vary.

Lesson 21
A
1. push-up
2. full-time
3. flight-test
4. high-speed
5. bluish-grey
6. go-between
7. fifty-yard-wide
8. highest-priced

B
1. b) first-rate
2. b) six-year-old
3. a) higher-up
4. a) three-year-old, b) ten-year-old
5. a) two-foot-long

C
Answers may vary, but should include that in the first sentence, Grandpa Smith was old and in the second sentence, the furniture was old.

Lesson 22
A
1. C: the weather is cooler, E: some plants become dormant
2. C: a dormant plant does not grow as much, E: it does not need as much water
3. C: you water the plant too much, E: you could drown the plant
4. C: gardeners put the plant in a cool place, E: the plant is fooled and becomes dormant
5. C: the plant is replaced in a warmer area, E: the plant blooms again

B
Phrases include: because of, as a result, thus, since, if, causes, so that, after

```
B E C A U S E O F
R E E S F C M L S
I L Q A W E T U P
N F V R F C H N S
O Y V E L T W U I
C A U S E S E G N
E S Z U K C B R C
B R P L H A U R E
E S O T H A T W S
```

C
Paragraphs will vary.

Lesson 23
A
1. adjective
2. infinitive, make
3. 1 - that oceans have rivers running through them OR 6 - which can help to make the water stay separate OR 8 - because the water came from a different part of the world

4. sentences include: 2, 3, 4, 5, 7, 9
5. phrases include: reason, help to make, because, cause
6. phrases include: on a permanently fixed course, through the rest, of the water, in the water, in temperature, of ocean water, from a different part, of the world, of temperature changes

B
1. self-propelling
2. compound
3. tem/per/a/ture
4. on land, in the ocean, in one area, of the same temperature
5. sentence 3, to help
6. Sentences will vary.
7. for, in
8. eleven years old, ex-sailor

Lesson 24
1. A
2. D
3. C
4. B
5. D
6. D
7. A
8. B
9. A
10. C

Unit 4
Lesson 25
A
1. Past, was making
2. Past, were experimenting
3. Present, is planning
4. Future, will be going
5. Present, am learning
6. Future, will be making
7. Past, was looking
8. Present, am trying
9. Present, is driving
10. Future, will be racing

B
Answer should include a helping verb and the -ing form of the main verb.

C
Sentences will vary. Verb form given.
1. was (were) flying
2. is (am) flying
3. will be flying
4. was (were) looking
5. is (am) looking
6. will be looking

Lesson 26
A
1. more magnetic
2. biggest
3. slower
4. longer
5. densest
6. thinner
7. tiniest
8. most unusual
9. more extreme
10. more interesting

B
1. best
2. worse
3. least
4. far
5. more

C
Sentences will vary.

Advantage Grammar Grade 5 © 2005 Creative Teaching Press

Lesson 27

A
1. a) P, b) A
2. a) A, b) P
3. a) P, b) A
4. a) A, b) P

B
1. A
2. P
3. P
4. A

C
Answer may include that passive sentences always contain helping verbs.

D
Answers will vary. Sample answers given.
1. Mars has the largest volcano and the longest canyon in the Solar System.
2. Scientists do not know if the Mars ice caps are ice made with water.
3. Two moons circle Mars.

Lesson 28

A
1. My, John Glenn
3. Uncle Ray
3. Ray
4. Dad
5. Most
6. Doctor David Wolf
7. Most NASA, Air Force
8. Perhaps Astronaut Carlos Noriega, Glenn School

B
1. sun
2. earth
3. Moon
4. Earth
5. Sun
6. moon

C
Sentences will vary.

Lesson 29

A
1. red
2. there
3. through
4. threw
5. they're
6. read
7. it's
8. their
9. its

B
List may include: blew-blue, plane - plain, mane - main, cents - sense, to - too- two, write - right - rite, be - bee, see - sea, rain - reign, might - mite, etc.

C
Sentences will vary.

Lesson 30

A
Circled words should include: in common, different, both, although, but, each

B
These facts should be in the circle for Saturn: Saturn has bright rings, Saturn looks yellow from Earth.
These facts should be in the circle for Uranus: has dark rings, no one knows what color it is.
These facts should be in the intersection of circles: large planets, have rings, space probes have passed the planet

C
Paragraphs will vary.

Lesson 31

A
1. sentence 3. Anyone can see five planets at night without using a telescope.
2. Part of the reason it's possible to see a planet on a certain night is because of its orbit
3. further, harder
4. sentence 6 - Sun
5. sentence 1 - has been looking

B
1. their - there
2. The light reflected from a planet has a shorter distance than the light from a star.
3. Only two things are being compared, so the phrase should be "more rapid."
4. So when you are sitting outside with your mom or dad a clear night, try to find a planet among the stars.
5. difference, shorter (more short), stronger, better, more rapid (most rapid)
6. Answers will vary. Sample answers given:
Alike: both shine in the sky at night, both move across the sky
Different: light from planets come shorter distances, move at different paces across the sky, light from planets is stronger, lights from stars twinkle, stars make a pattern in the sky

Lesson 32
1. D
2. F
3. B
4. F
5. D
6. H
7. D
8. H
9. B
10. H

Unit 5
Lesson 33

A
ordered: part of speech, word, word it describes
1. adj-funny-poems
2. adv-outrageously, adj-funny-he
3. adj-golden-tales
4. adj-some-beans, adj-magic-beans
5. adj-daring-acrobats, adj-high-up-trapeze
6. adv-secretly-spied
7. adv-swiftly-sank, adv-suddenly-sank
8. adv-quite-soggy, adj-soggy-children

Answer Key

B
Sentences will vary.

C
Sentences will vary.

Lesson 34
A
ordered: singular/plural, subject, predicate
1. S -book- is
2. P- two brothers and two sisters -discover
3. S-lion-is
4. P-animals-talk and think
5. P-trees-are

B
1. become
2. greets
3. seems
4. love
5. were
6. welcomes
7. does
8. explain

C
1. is
2. are
3. want
4. enjoy
5. reads
6. is
7. tells
8. contains
9. likes
10. retells

Lesson 35
A
Sentences will vary. Sample answers given:
1. Karana clothed herself in furs and feathers.
2. Wolves killed Little Ramos.
3. O'Dell penned more historical fiction novels.
4. O'Dell can add the Newberry Award to his awards for writing this book.

B
Sentences will vary. Sample answers given:
1. Scott O'Dell wrote many other good books.
2. He wrote one book about my area of the country.
3. People in the area were afraid they were cursed.
4. The Black Pearl tells about divers collecting pearls.
5. This book may be the best book about our area.
6. The book could have been written about someone my grandfather knew.

Lesson 36
A
1. From the Mixed-up Files of Mrs. Basil E. Frankweiler.
2. "Angel."
3. none
4. The Wall Street Journal, New York Times and Daily News.
5. "The greatest movie ever."
6. Shrek.
7. "Hallelujah,"
8. Loser "Win."

9. Reader's Digest "Humor in Uniform."
10. Friendship

B
Answers will vary.

C
Answers will vary.

Lesson 37
A
1. les'-sən
2. in'-stənt
3. ə-lone'
4. au'-təmn
5. rel'-ə-tive
6. cən-tain'
7. bis'-cət
8. min'-ə-mum
9. mag nət
10. so'/fə

B
Only circled items are listed:
2, 3, 4, 7, 8, 10

C
Sample answers given:
spelled a: adult, instant, alone, sofa, final
spelled e: magnet, father, label, keeper
spelled i: charity, minimum, fossil
spelled o: solemn, lesson, contain, person
spelled u: autumn, biscuit, hurry

Lesson 38
A
1. The first sentence is the topic sentence.
2. It is interesting on many levels (Doldrums example).
3. The word plays are fun (Which example).
4. It's a great adventure.
5. The last sentence is the restatement.

B
Paragraphs will vary, but should be written in reverse order.

Lesson 39
A
1. The book title should be underlined - including in the heading.
2. 2, 8
3. Books with a girl main character don't always interest me. OR I'm not always interested in books with girl main characters.
4. good, girl, main, great, science, fiction, time, space, real, realistic, interesting
5. most important point first
6. Best: Juan likes science fiction; Second: The family seemed real; Third: The characters were interesting

Advantage Grammar Grade 5 © 2005 Creative Teaching Press

B

The book should be underlined and the chapter title should be in quotation marks as follows: "The Transparent Column."

2. The word travels should be travel because it is a plural (compound) subject.

3. Sample answer: However, four chapters are still to come!

4. very-weird, actually-find, still-are, now-will stop

5. teenage-girl, weird-ladies, quirky-brother, transparent -column, four-chapters

6. circled words: cen'-tərs, ə-round', fa'-thər, tra'-vəls, trans-par'- ənt, col'- əmn

Lesson 40

1. C	6. G
2. H	7. B
3. A	8. H
4. J	
5. D	

Unit 6

Lesson 41

A

1. DO	6. ID
2. ID	7. ID
3. DO	8. DO
4. DO	9. DO
5. DO	10. ID

B

Answers will vary but may include placement in the sentence or the fact that there is never an indirect object unless there's also a direct object.

C

ordered: subject, direct object, indirect object
1. I, new trading cards, myself
2. My friends and I, them
3. We, presents, each other
4. hobby
5. Mom, us
6. She, cookies and lemonade, the club

D

1. me
2. She
3. us
4. We
5. they
6. them

Lesson 42

A

1. the bass player, Kathleen
2. comp, accompany
3. Mostly seventh- and eighth-graders, the other members
4. The Fresh Men, a high school rock band
5. sax, a saxophone player
6. improv, make up my own solo on the spot
7. the trombone section, the 'bones
8. Joshua Redman, a sax player, my new favorite musician

B

Answers will vary but may include the placement in the sentence and punctuation, such as commas or parentheses.

C

Answers will vary.

Lesson 43

A

Terms may vary (such as subject or noun).
1. subject, helping verb, negative adverb, predicate
2. possessive pronoun, subject, helping verb, negative adverb, predicate
3. negative contraction subject predicate prepositional phrase
4. negative contraction subject predicate adverb

B

Answers may vary. Sample answers given.
1. Between the helping verb and the predicate.
2. A contraction is used before the subject, which comes before the predicate.

C

Answers may vary. Sample answers given.
1. don't
2. rarely
3. Can't
4. hardly
5. Don't

D

1. inactive - not active
2. discomfort - not comfortable
3. nonstop - without stopping
4. uninformed - not informed
5. antipollution - against pollution

E

Sentences will vary.

Lesson 44

A

1. FE	4. NMI
2. FE	5. NMI
3. NMI	6. FE

B

1. 9).	4. boyfriend)
2. Area).	5. guides)
3. Branch)	

C

1. 1) 2) 3)
2. (by S. Ray).
3. (Lloyd George).
4. (chapter 1).
5. (1) (2) (3) (4) (5)

D

1. (the author is Thomas Rampton).
2. (Ingram).
3. (1) (2)
4. (the Colorado).
5. (or just look from above it).

Answer Key

Lesson 45

A
1. dessert
2. whether
3. passed
4. vary
5. course
6. have
7. desert
8. past
9. weather
10. of
11. very
12. coarse

B
1. nobody
2. may be
3. every day
4. No body
5. everyday
6. Maybe

C
Sentences will vary.

Lesson 46

A
Sentences will vary.

B
Paragraphs will vary.

Lesson 47

A
1. change everyday to every day
2. 5   hay).
3. me
4. change passed to past
5. 5, Dave renames
6. not, doesn't, never
7. Sentences will vary.
8. the pond and the barn

B
1. vary - very
2. 3, (c)
3. breakfast
4. us
5. 1, my tribe
6. Sentences will vary.
7. Sentences will vary.

Lesson 48
1. C
2. J
3. B
4. H
5. D
6. J
7. A
8. H
9. B

Test Practice
1. A
2. H
3. D
4. G
5. B
6. J
7. D
8. G
9. D
10. F
11. B
12. G
13. A
14. J
15. C
16. G
17. D
18. G
19. C
20. F
21. C

Advantage Grammar Grade 5 © 2005 Creative Teaching Press

Orchard Books, 95 Madison Avenue, New York, NY 10016

Manufactured in the United States of America. Printed by Barton Press, Inc.
Bound by Horowitz/Rae. Book design by Mina Greenstein.
The text of this book is set in 20 point Veljovic Book.
The illustrations are watercolor reproduced in full color. 10 9 8 7 6 5 4 3 2 1

Library of Congress Cataloging-in-Publication Data
Bassède, Francine. [Boutique de Georges à la plage. English]
George's store at the shore / by Francine Bassède. — 1st American ed.   p. cm.
Summary: George and Mary bring out items to sell at George's store at the beach, counting from
one to ten as they set out the merchandise.
ISBN O-531-30083-8 (trade: alk. paper)—ISBN 0-531-33083-4 (lib. bdg. : alk. paper)
[1. Stores, Retail—Fiction. 2. Seashore—Fiction. 3. Counting.] I. Title.
PZ7.B29285Ge 1998 [E]—dc21 97-38282

GEORGE'S STORE
at the SHORE

by Francine Bassède

Orchard Books / New York

All summer long,
George gets up early.
He must get his store
at the beach ready,
with the help of his
friend, Mary.

First he carries
an umbrella. Mary
props it against the
door of the shop.

Next, two nets,
very useful for
catching fish,
crabs, and
sea urchins.

3

One, two...
One, two...
One, two, three
ducky floaty things:
green, blue, and red.

George brings four
beach balls, and Mary
arranges them on the
floor of the store.

"Mary, watch your claws,"
he warns.

Next, five striped
sailor shirts of cotton,
soft and cool.

6

What a balancing act!
George brings six pails.
Mary arranges them
on the top shelf.

A hat is indispensable
at the beach. Mary
hangs seven for
the shop.

Eight shovels for
making deep holes and
tall sand castles.

A glass of freshly
squeezed orange juice!
Very tasty in the fresh sea air—
there are nine.

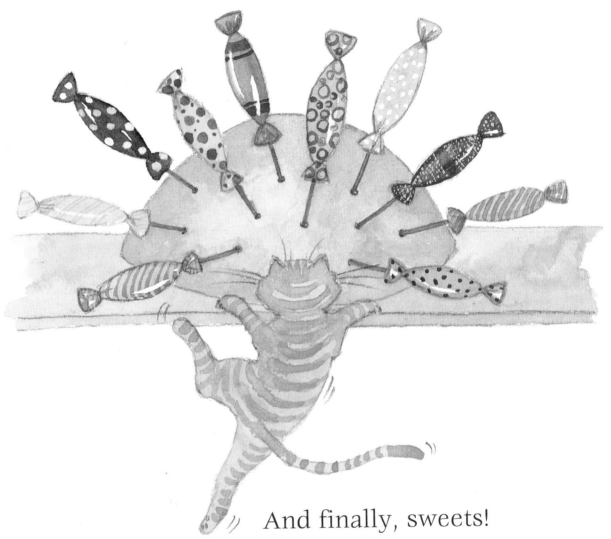

And finally, sweets!
Ten lollipops, useful while daydreaming,
each a different flavor: strawberry, lemon,
mint, chocolate, caramel, licorice, honey,
apricot, raspberry, and black currant.

A fine assortment.

The store is open.
George and Mary
are ready. It won't
be long before
customers arrive!